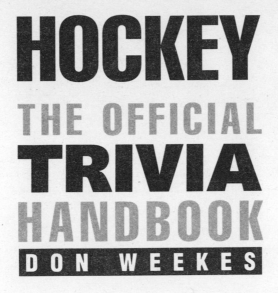

HOCKEY
THE OFFICIAL
TRIVIA
HANDBOOK
DON WEEKES

GREYSTONE
BOOKS

Douglas & McIntyre
Vancouver/Toronto

D0357654

For Caroline

Copyright © 1993 by Don Weekes

  95 96 97   5 4 3

All rights reserved. No part of this book may be reproduced or transmitted in any form by any means without permission in writing from the publisher, except by a reviewer, who may quote brief passages in a review.

Greystone Books
A division of Douglas & McIntyre Ltd.
1615 Venables Street
Vancouver, British Columbia V5L 2H1

Canadian Cataloguing in Publication Data

Weekes, Don.
  Hockey : the official trivia handbook

ISBN 1-55054-092-0

1. Hockey — Miscellanea. 2. National Hockey League — Miscellanea. I. Title.
GV847.W432 1993   796.962   C93-091450-3

Editing by Maja Grip
Design by Eric Ansley & Associates Ltd.
Typesetting by Vancouver Desktop Publishing Centre
Cover photo by S. Reyes/Bruce Bennett Studios

Printed and bound in Canada by Webcom
Printed on acid-free paper ∞

Don Weekes is a Montreal television writer and producer with CFCF-TV's nationally syndicated sports magazine, "Hockey World." His work has been broadcast on a number of American sports cable networks, including PASS in Detroit, Prime Ticket in Los Angeles and PRISM in Philadelphia.

CONTENTS

PREFACE

Although this handbook contains hundreds of relevant hockey facts that will surprise even the hard-core fan, it's not the kind of sports quiz book that will over-challenge or bore the casual spectator with statistics and facts. Nor does it simply test memory or require an NHL stat sheet to answer the questions, crosswords and games. And you needn't ever have laced up a pair of skates to figure out: How many goals are usually scored in an NHL game? Who is Freddy Charles? or How much did Mark Messier pay in fines for sticking Ulf Samuelsson?

You need only an interest in hockey (and a sharp pencil). Because the questions are multiple-choice, every fan has a fighting chance on every one, no matter what his or her level of strength on the subject. And each answer offers intriguing and unusual insights seldom found in one single reference. For example, what area of the rink gets shortened when the ice surface is less than regulation size? In the Tie Domi–Bob Probert "Heavyweight Fight," who won? How many punches were thrown? And how many hit their mark?

For convenience, all answers follow the questions at the end of each chapter. (Hey! No cheating!) Between each chapter are hockey crossword puzzles, quizzes and games, all designed to rattle your confidence and test your true knowledge of the game. (Information is current to the June '93 NHL draft.)

★ ★ ★

If hockey ever had a rapper, it would have to be Danny Gallivan, the late Montreal Canadiens broadcaster who invented and introduced such words as *cannonading* and *spin-a-rama* into hockey's play-by-play repertoire. His colourful phrasings, his voice and his enthusiasm elevated the game and its tempo to new emotional heights. Danny didn't really *announce* a game, he *rapped* it, spitting out words (some of which we had never heard before) as fast as the action progressed, mixing the language of hockey with his unique broadcast style.

Danny simply made hockey more thrilling. I'll never forget my sister Karen's first visit to the Montreal Forum. Once she got used to the slope of the arena stands and the game had begun, she called out, "Where's Danny?", feeling cheated that the voice of the Canadiens was absent from the live event. Today, we all feel that way.

Thanks for the thrills, Danny. You're a true champion.

DON WEEKES
June 1993

1

THE OPENING FACE-OFF

Before the opening face-off at important games in Philadelphia's Spectrum, the Flyers play Kate Smith's stirring rendition of "God Bless America" for inspiration. Since the tradition began in 1972, Ms. Smith's win-loss record is 63–13–3. Get inspired. In this first quiz, your faith could be called into question.

(Answers are on page 5)

1.1 **What is the average number of goals scored (by both teams) per NHL game today?**
   A. 6 to 7
   B. 7 to 8
   C. 8 to 9
   D. More than 9

1.2 **Who is the NHL's all-time leading point getter among U.S.-born players?**
   A. Neal Broten
   B. Phil Housley
   C. Pat LaFontaine
   D. Joe Mullen

1.3 **What proportion of Jets goals did Teemu Selanne score in 1992–93, his rookie season?**
   A. 1 in 3
   B. 1 in 4
   C. 1 in 5
   D. 1 in 6

1.4 According to *Sports Illustrated*, what is the most unbeatable record in all of sports?
A. Wayne Gretzky's single-season point total
B. Bobby Orr's career point total
C. Glenn Hall's consecutive-game streak
D. The Montreal Canadiens' Stanley Cup-winning record

1.5 Who is the NHL's all-time most consistent +30-goal scorer?
A. Mike Gartner
B. Bobby Hull
C. Phil Esposito
D. Wayne Gretzky

1.6 Which NHLer has received the most penalty minutes in one game?
A. Dave "Tiger" Williams
B. Tie Domi
C. Randy Holt
D. Basil McRae

1.7 How did Phil Esposito come up with the name "Lightning" for the Tampa Bay franchise?
A. He held a promotional contest in Tampa Bay.
B. Tampa Bay is "the lightning capital of the world."
C. A lightning bolt almost struck him.
D. He named it after his lightning-quick wrist shot.

1.8 Which NHLer played the most years with his original team?
A. The Bruins' Ray Bourque
B. The Hawks' Keith Brown
C. The Jets' Thomas Steen
D. The Kings' Dave Taylor

1.9 Which hockey play-by-play announcer says, after a goal is scored, "He beat that goalie like a rented mule," or "Buy Sam a drink, and get his dog one, too"?
   A. Fred Cusick of WSBK in Boston
   B. Jim Robson of CKNW in Vancouver
   C. Mike Lange of KDKA in Pittsburgh
   D. Mike Emrick of WPHL in Philadelphia

1.10 How much did Buffalo's Grant Fuhr earn tending goal in 1992–93?
   A. $10,000 to $15,000 per game
   B. $15,000 to $20,000 per game
   C. $20,000 to $25,000 per game
   D. More than $25,000 per game

1.11 Who has the hardest slapshot in the NHL?
   A. Brett Hull
   B. Al Iafrate
   C. Al MacInnis
   D. Mike Modano

1.12 What is the average effectiveness of the power play?
   A. 15%
   B. 18%
   C. 21%
   D. 24%

1.13 Since Canada Cup competition began, which player has racked up the highest point totals?
   A. Mark Messier
   B. Sergei Makarov
   C. Wayne Gretzky
   D. Vladimir Krutov

1.14 How many French Canadiens played on the Quebec Nordiques in 1992–93?
A. 4
B. 8
C. 10
D. 12

1.15 When the ice surface in NHL arenas, like Boston Garden or Buffalo Memorial Auditorium, is less than the regulation 200-foot length, what area of the rink is shortened?
A. The 11 feet between the boards and the goal lines
B. The 60 feet between the goal lines and the blue lines
C. The 58 feet between the blue lines
D. Each rink area is reduced proportionately.

1.16 On average, how many hockey sticks will a player use up during a regular season?
A. Fewer than 100
B. 100 to 200
C. 200 to 300
D. More than 300

1.17 What two NHLers cameoed in the film *The Mighty Ducks*?
A. Basil McRae and Mike Modano
B. Basil McRae and Dave Gagner
C. Basil McRae and Mark Tinordi
D. Basil McRae and Russ Courtnall

1.18 What is the approximate percentage breakdown of Canadian, American and non–North American players in the NHL?

A. 80% Canadian, 10% American, 10% non–North American

B. 66% Canadian, 17% American, 17% non–North American

C. 66% Canadian, 10% American, 24% non–North American

D. 50% Canadian, 25% American, 25% non–North American

THE OPENING FACE-OFF
Answers

1.1 B. 7 to 8 goals.
NHL teams averaged 7.3 goals per game (or 7311 tallies in 1008 matches) in 1992–93, an increase of half a goal per game over the previous season's average of 6.9 goals. Many factors are involved, but this jump is consistent with past increases, all occurring during expansion years: in 1970–71, scoring jumped from 5.8 to 6.2 goals; in 1972–73, from 6.1 to 6.6; and in 1974–75, from 6.4 to 6.9.

1.2 D. Joe Mullen.
Mullen grew up in one of the U.S.'s toughest 'hoods, Hell's Kitchen in New York, where physical skills and street smarts were tactical prerequisites for staying alive, even in the area's playgrounds. It was there that Mullen picked up his rugged style and team spirit, playing roller hockey against his brothers and best friends before joining the Metropolitan Junior Hockey League, an outfit

formed by Emile Francis to help the area's street kids stay out of trouble. Sports literally kept Mullen alive. After winning a scholarship to Boston College, he signed with St. Louis in 1979. Three teams, three Stanley Cups and seven 40-goal seasons later, Mullen ranks first among all American-born NHLers.

AMERICA'S BEST NHL PLAYERS			
Player	Years	Games	Points
1. J. Mullen	12	842	919
2. P. Housley	11	840	817
3. P. LaFontaine	10	671	807
4. N. Broten	12	876	796
5. D. Christian	14	1000	770
6. M. Howe	14	867	712
Current to 1992–93			

1.3 B. 1 in 4.
In his first NHL season, Selanne was responsible for 24% of the Jets' total offensive output, scoring 76 of Winnipeg's 322 goals in 1992–93, probably the highest goal ratio ever achieved by a rookie.

1.4 C. Glenn Hall's consecutive-game streak.
After analyzing the greatest records in professional sports, including Ty Cobb's .367 career batting average, the Boston Celtics' eight straight NBA championships and Jack Nicklaus's 20 major golf championships, *Sports Illustrated* listed Hall's 502 consecutive complete games as the most unbreakable record in sports. From 1955 through 1962, in seven complete seasons with Detroit and Chicago, the maskless Hall never missed a start. While 502 is his regular-season total, the figure increases to 551 when Hall's 49 playoff games are included. As *SI* notes, Hall holds "the record of records...that won't ever be broken," especially with teams carrying two goalies

now, the 84-game schedule and the extended playoff format. But his iron-man mark shouldn't be dismissed as just a product of his era. The quality of Hall's play throughout his streak earned him NHL Rookie of the Year honours in 1956 and won the Blackhawks a surprise Stanley Cup in 1961, as well as ensuring Hall a place on six All-Star teams. Hall's astonishing record ended on November 7, 1962. He had strained his back at practice while fastening a toe strap. The next night, midway through the first period, the pain was so severe Hall removed himself from play.

1.5 A. Mike Gartner.
Hull, Esposito and Gretzky each recorded 13 straight +30-goal seasons, but Gartner has gone them one better, earning his 14th consecutive +30-goal season in 1992–93. Gartner has scored at least 33 goals in each of those 14 seasons and has hit the 40-goal plateau eight times. After potting 45 goals in 1992–93, the 33-year-old forward moved into sixth place on the NHL's all-time scoring list, between Mike Bossy and Bobby Hull.

1.6 C. Randy Holt.
It was during a Flyers-Kings brawl on March 11, 1979, that nine NHL penalty records were set, three of them by Holt, who was assessed a record 67 minutes for nine penalties, all during a wild first period that ended with a 12-minute melee that carried across the ice to the Los Angeles bench. Referee Wally Harris ejected 10 players, five from each team, and handed out 352 penalty minutes, including one minor, three majors, two 10-minute misconducts and a triple game misconduct to Holt.

1.7 C. A lightning bolt almost struck him.
Yes, Tampa Bay *is* "the lightning capital of the world," but that wasn't good enough for Esposito. He needed to be thunderstruck. And that's what happened one summer

afternoon in 1990 when a bolt struck very close to his restaurant table overlooking Tampa Bay. Stunned by the loud boom, Esposito looked around, and an old woman next to him immediately suggested that he should name his "ice hockey" team the Lightning. That's all Espo needed. He received conditional franchise approval in December, and a year later the Lightning were as real as the thunderstorms over Tampa Bay.

1.8 D. The Kings' Dave Taylor.

It's not often that a lowly 15th-round draft pick makes it to the big leagues, and if he does, it's almost certain he won't stay very long. Enter Dave Taylor, who was chosen very late (210th) in the 1975 entry draft and who defied the odds and NHL Central Scouting by sticking around long after even the top picks had vanished from the rosters. As our front cover depicts, the Kings got a tireless worker, every shift, every game.

THE NHL'S TOP 6 "SAME TEAM" VETERANS				
Player	Team	Years	Games	Points
1. D. Taylor	LA	16	1078	1062
2. R. Bourque	Bos	14	1028	1097
3. S. Larmer	Chi	13	891	923
4. N. Broten	Stars	13	876	796
5. T. Steen	Winn	12	843	751
6. K. Brown	Chi	14	812	330
Current to 1992–93				

1.9 C. Mike Lange of KDKA in Pittsburgh.

Lange's trademark is his quirky, off-the-wall expressions, which Penguins fans know by heart. When Pittsburgh is winning late in the game, Lange calls out, "Ladies and gentlemen, Elvis has just left the building," or another Lange classic, "Get in the fast lane, Grandma, the bingo game's about to start."

1.10 D. More than $25,000 per game.
Fuhr's base salary of $1.6 million divided by 84 games equals $19,047 per game, but Fuhr actually played only 54 games in 1992–93, thus earning $29,629.63 every time he stepped onto the ice to backstop either Toronto or Buffalo. That figure does not include the $2,000 per win guaranteed by his contract for victories 20 through 30, or playoff bonus money geared to the number of games played per round. Fuhr went 24–24–6 in 1992–93.

1.11 B. Al Iafrate.
In terms of sheer velocity, Iafrate's shot is considered the League's hardest. In the skills competition during the 1993 All-Star weekend, Iafrate's howitzer was clocked at 105.2 miles per hour. Shooting left, he used a Koho Revolution 2240 stick with a curve near the heel of the blade to finish well ahead of runner-up Modano, who blasted a 101.6 mph shot. But the question of who has the hardest boomer in game situations is far from settled. Goalies around the League are convinced that distinction belongs to others like Brett Hull or Al MacInnis.

1.12 C. 21%.
In the last eight NHL seasons, each team averaged about 370 power play opportunities per year, resulting in 76 goals, a 20.6% success rate. The figures vary from season to season and with each team, but the most productive clubs score on the man advantage 23% of the time (and as high as 26% at home). From 1987 through 1990, the Calgary Flames recorded one of the highest success rates, averaging 31%, or a goal in every three power play situations.

1.13 C. Wayne Gretzky.
Gretzky, then a 15-year-old junior sensation, watched from the stands when the world's best players competed in the first Canada Cup in 1976. Five years later, he was playing

his Canadian heart out against Czechs, Finns and Russians. With four Canada Cups (1981/84/87/91) under his belt, the Great One truly ranks as the greatest in the world, thanks to his 57 points (17 goals, 40 assists) in 31 games.

THE ALL-TIME CANADA CUP POINT LEADERS			
Player	Team	Games	Points
1. W. Gretzky	Canada Nat.	31	57
2. S. Makarov	Soviet Nat.	22	31
3. V. Krutov	Soviet Nat.	22	30
4. M. Messier	Canada Nat.	31	26

1.14 A. 4 players.
Only four Quebec regulars — Steve Duchesne, Steven Finn, Stephane Fiset and Claude Lapointe — can claim French as a first language. It's the "United Nations" Nordiques — sans Eric Lindros but with four Russians, a Czech, a Swede and a hand-picked group of English Canadian players. With nine new members on a roster of 20, Quebec iced the best road team in 1992–93 with a 24–10–8 record.

1.15 C. The 58 feet between the blue lines.
Until new arenas are built in Boston and Buffalo, NHL teams will continue to play in smaller neutral zones between the blue lines. For example, because Boston Garden's ice surface (191' x 83') is short by nine feet, the neutral zone is reduced to 49 feet. In the past, teams like the Bruins drafted players and developed playing systems around their smaller rinks, believing it was to their advantage, with 40 home games, to use bangers like Terry O'Reilly to create tight checking games by grinding down speedy forwards in the smaller neutral zone. Shrinking the areas behind the nets or between the goal lines and blue lines would drastically alter the play of the game in the attacking and defending zones.

1.16 D. More than 300.
It depends on the player, but most NHLers use around 30 dozen (360) hockey sticks each season. While some players change sticks simply in hopes of ending a bad streak, the common reason is shaft breakage. Defensemen tend to go through the most sticks, incurring frequent breakages from blueline slapshots or from tight checking around the net. Although aluminum-shafted sticks have made inroads, white ash is still the preferred choice for the balance, lightness and stiffness it offers.

1.17 A. Basil McRae and Mike Modano.
Disney scored big bucks at the box office in 1992 with *The Might Ducks*, the story of a team of peewee misfits reluctantly coached by one Gordon Bombay, played by Emilio Estevez. Under Bombay, the Ducks gel into a winning team featuring two girls, a black-and-white threesome known as "the Oreo Line" and an on-ice manoeuvre called "the Flying V." On the road to victory, Bombay confronts his hockey past and introduces Basil McRae and Mike Modano to the team. Modano's only line is uninspiring, unlike his tremendous shot and stick-handling skills in real life. Hey, Mike, don't give up your day job. Quack! Quack!

1.18 B. 66% Canadian, 17% American, 17% non–North American.
In 1992–93, 66.2% of League players were Canadian-born, 16.6% were American and 17.2% were from outside North America, including the 46 Russian NHLers. During expansion in 1967–68, 96.7% of the League's 270 players were Canadian, 2.0% were American and 1.3% non–North American.

Across

1. & 18 Across: S.B. is Jets #14
3. _____ Probert
5. Penguins #22, tough winger, init.
7. Quebec's #28, defense, init.
9. Calgary's Joe _____
12. Boston's _____ Oates
13. Rangers centre Ed _____
16. Czech _____ Ruzicka
17. Mark Messier's nickname
18. See 1 Across
20. Tampa sniper Petr _____
22. Quebec's _____ Nolan
24. Geoff's brother, init.
25. Jets #38, centre, init.
27. Islanders #10 (1992-93), Claude _____
30. Habs #47, Stephane _____
33. Brett _____
34. Old centre Keith _____
36. Penguins #55, init.
39. Oilers #34 (1992-93), init.
40. Caps #34, Al _____
43. Quebec's Martin _____
46. Habs #25/top scorer in 1992-93, init.
48. Stars #22, Swede, init.
49. Sabres Dale _____
51. Hawks #27, sniper, init.
53. Leafs #14, sniper, init.
54. Goalie Jeff _____
55. Boston's Cam _____
56. Sharks' first captain, Doug _____

Down

1. Old Soviet, Anatoli _____
2. Mr. Dirty, _____ Samuelsson
3. Rod _____ 'Amour
4. Extra period, abbr.
6. Oilers #18, Craig _____
7. Quebec's Mats _____
8. Oilers #39, centre, init.
10. Islanders #27, _____ King
11. Brothers John and Dan _____
12. Old Soviet defenseman, Devils #7 (1992-93), init.
14. Brothers Paul and Gino _____
15. Old Hab, _____ Cournoyer
17. Canuck goalie Kirk _____
18. Ottawa goalie Craig _____
19. Flames #26, Robert _____
21. Kings "Lucky Luc," init.
23. Flyers #88, init.
26. Jets #35, goalie, init.
28. Flyers #9, Pelle _____
29. _____ Tikkanen
31. "The Eagle" Ed _____
32. Kevin or Scott _____
35. Devils #31, goalie, init.
37. Quebec #9, ex-Flyer, init.
38. Rangers #8, US-born centre, init.
41. Sabres Soviet sniper, init.
42. Sabres #12, Bob _____
44. Jets #5, Soviet, init.
45. Ottawa #4, Brad _____
47. Flyers #33, goalie, init.
50. Devils #3, _____ Daneyko
52. Leafs #4, defense, init.

CROSSWORD #1

STARTING LINE-UP

(Solution is on page 118)

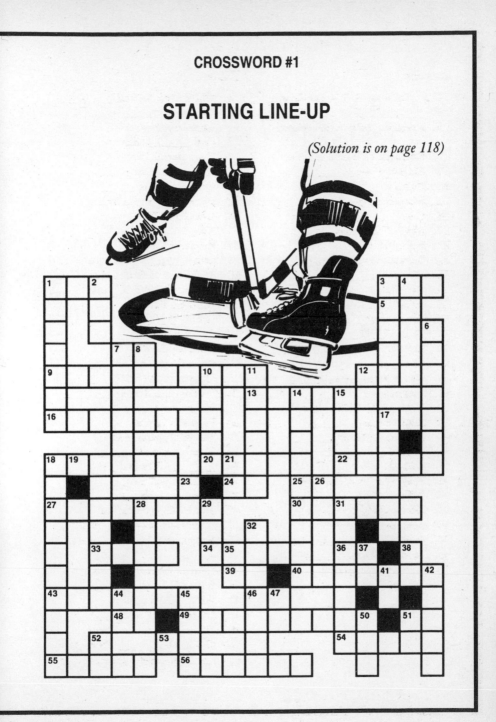

2

FIRSTS AND LASTS

Sometimes player or team statistics are overlooked in favour of their more unusual achievements. Take Ralph Bowman. A two-time Stanley Cup winner with Detroit, Bowman was your solid stay-at-home defenseman until December 4, 1934, when, as a member of the all-but-forgotten St. Louis Eagles, he beat Alex Connell one on one to score the NHL's first penalty shot. Here are some other firsts and lasts worth checking out.

(Answers are on page 17)

2.1 When were NHL divisions *last* named geographically (i.e., Eastern, Western, etc.)?
A. 1967–68
B. 1970–71
C. 1973–74
D. 1979–80

2.2 Who was the first player to jump directly from high school to the NHL?
A. Brian Lawton
B. Bobby Carpenter
C. Tom Barrasso
D. Phil Housley

2.3 **Name the last NHL goalie to play every minute of every game of an entire regular season.**
A. Glenn Hall, Chicago, 1961–62
B. Eddie Johnston, Boston, 1963–64
C. Bernie Parent, Philadelphia, 1973–74
D. Grant Fuhr, Edmonton, 1987–88

2.4 **Even though Wayne Gretzky is famous for his playmaking behind the opponents' net, he wasn't the first to do it. Who was?**
A. Bryan Trottier
B. Bobby Clarke
C. Ken Hodge
D. Jacques Lemaire

2.5 **When was the last time a referee called a penalty to one team in overtime in the Stanley Cup finals?**
A. 1950
B. 1980
C. 1990
D. It's never happened.

2.6 **Name the first NHL team to reach 100 points in a season.**
A. The old Ottawa Senators
B. The Montreal Canadiens
C. The Toronto Maple Leafs
D. The Detroit Red Wings

2.7 **When did a regular-position player last tend goal during an NHL game?**
A. 1960
B. 1970
C. 1980
D. 1990

2.8 **Who first suggested that face masks be mandatory equipment?**
A. A goalie
B. A scoring leader
C. A general manager
D. An equipment manager

2.9 **Who scored the last WHA goal?**
A. Mark Messier
B. Wayne Gretzky
C. Dave Semenko
D. Bobby Hull

2.10 **When was the last time a goalie played an entire All-Star game?**
A. Jacques Plante in 1955
B. Glenn Hall in 1965
C. Ken Dryden in 1975
D. John Vanbiesbrouck in 1985

2.11 **Which NHL club was the first to travel regularly by airplane?**
A. The Boston Bruins
B. The Los Angeles Kings
C. The Chicago Blackhawks
D. The Toronto Maple Leafs

FIRSTS AND LASTS
Answers

2.1 C. 1973-74.

NHL divisions haven't been identified by geographical location since 1973–74, when the League's 16 teams made up the Eastern and Western divisions. In 1993–94, the old Smythe, Norris, Adams and Patrick divisions become the fan-friendly Pacific, Central, Northeast and Atlantic divisions, divided into the Western and Eastern conferences.

2.2 B. Bobby Carpenter.

One of the most highly touted American amateur players ever, Carpenter made the cover of *Sports Illustrated* while still in high school at St. John's Prep in Massachusetts. Carpenter proved Washington had drafted wisely (first pick, third overall) by notching his first point 12 seconds into his NHL debut and scoring his first goal before the night was out. Carpenter earned 32 goals and 67 points in his rookie season in 1981–82, a Capitals record. Housley (1982), Lawton (1983) and Barrasso (1983) also jumped from high school into the NHL.

2.3 B. Eddie Johnston, Boston, 1963–64.

Although Grant Fuhr holds the NHL record for most games played in one season (75 games in 1987–88), the last time a goalie played an *entire* season was 30 years ago. Johnston played every minute of every game for the Boston Bruins during the 70-game schedule in 1963–64. Backing him up were a couple of kids named Gerry Cheevers and Bernie Parent.

2.4 B. Bobby Clarke.

According to Gretzky, Clarke was the first NHLer to play behind the opposing team's net, using it to set up his slotman or deking out either end to make a pass or score on a wrap-around. Gretzky first tried it when he was 14 and playing against 19-year-olds in Junior B. Seeing the way Gretzky was being slammed around in front of the net, coach Gene Popeil suggested he play behind it, just like Clarke. Gretzky discovered that the net functioned almost like another player to protect him. The Islanders' Bryan Trottier also played with great effectiveness behind the opponents' net.

2.5 B. 1980.

An overtime power play last occurred during the finals on May 13, 1980, when the Flyers' Jim Watson was assessed two minutes for holding. With just one second remaining in the power play, Denis Potvin scored on Pete Peeters to give the Islanders a 4–3 victory over Philadelphia in Game 1. The referee was Andy vanHellemond.

2.6 D. The Detroit Red Wings.

If you took the best goalie of the day and added the NHL's top forward line and scoring leader to a solid defense corps, you'd have a team like the Red Wings of the 1950s. Terry Sawchuk, Gordie Howe, Syd Abel and Ted Lindsay produced the League's dominant force from 1948 through 1955, despite some extraordinary competition. Battling the Montreal and Toronto powerhouses, the Red Wings finished first a record seven seasons straight, won four Stanley Cups in six years and played the NHL's first 100-point season in 1950–51. In 1952, they became the first team to sweep the playoffs, winning in the minimum of eight games, including four shutouts at the Olympia in Detroit.

2.7 A. 1960.
Bruins forward Jerry Toppazzini was the last regular position player to tend goal in an NHL game, subbing for an injured Don Simmons in the last minute of a 4–1 loss to Detroit on October 6, 1960.

2.8 C. A general manager.
In 1947, concern over the rising number of goaltender injuries in the new 60-game schedule prompted Rangers manager Frank Boucher to recommend that goalies be required to wear face masks. Boucher's suggestion raised eyebrows throughout the League. Coaches were the most adamantly opposed, insisting that masks restricted a goalie's vision. More than a decade would pass before Jacques Plante defied everyone, including his coach and manager, by donning the NHL's first goalie mask.

2.9 C. Dave Semenko.
On May 20, 1979, the Oilers' Dave Semenko closed a chapter in hockey history, scoring the last WHA goal in a 7–3 loss to the Jets during the final Avco Cup playoff game between Edmonton and Winnipeg.

2.10 B. Glenn Hall in 1965.
Hall was the last goalie to backstop an entire All-Star game, beating the defending Stanley Cup champion Montreal Canadiens 5–2 in 1965.

2.11 A. The Boston Bruins.
With clubs now owning and chartering private jets, it's hard to imagine a 70-game schedule when all travel between NHL cities was done by train. At the time, the League had only six East Coast teams, but some trips lasted as long as 14 hours — until 1958, when the Bruins began flying regularly. Other clubs soon followed, ending hockey's long association with the Pullman sleeper car.

A TRIO OF STARS

There was Toronto's "Hound Line," so called because as teenagers they played together in Saskatchewan for the Notre Dame College Hounds. Over in Philadelphia, the "Crazy Eights" clicked with No. 88, No. 8 and No. 18. And in 1970–71, the "Nitro Line" exploded for a record 140 goals, 35% of the Bruins' total offensive production. Some forward lines are more special than others. And when they gel, a nickname for the trio is bound to find its way into hockey history, surviving long after the line has broken up.

Fill in the blanks with the missing linemates listed below.

(Answers are on page 115)

Trevor Linden	Christian Ruuttu
Ken Hodge	Luc Robitaille
Joe Juneau	Greg Gilbert
Ulf Nilsson	Cliff Ronning
Mike Bossy	Wayne Cashman
Clark Gillies	Brent Fedyk
Russ Courtnall	Adam Oates
Tomas Sandstrom	Anders Hedberg
Gary Leeman	Eric Lindros

Left Wing	Centre	Right Wing

1. Philadelphia's Crazy Eights, 1992–93:

		Mark Recchi
_____	_____	_____

2. New York Islanders' Grande Trio, 1979–80:

	Bryan Trottier	
_____	_____	_____

3. Toronto's Hound Line, 1983–84:

Wendel Clark		
_____	_____	_____

4. Boston's Bonanza Line, 1992–93:

		Dmitri Kvartalnov
_____	_____	_____

5. The WHA Winnipeg Jets Line, 1970s:

Bobby Hull		
_____	_____	_____

6. Los Angeles' WOW Line ("Without Wayne"), 1992–93:

	Jari Kurri	
_____	_____	_____

7. Chicago's Reject Line, 1992–93:

		Dirk Graham
_____	_____	_____

8. Vancouver's Life Line, 1991–92:

Geoff Courtnall		
_____	_____	_____

9. Boston's Nitro Line, 1970–71:

	Phil Esposito	
_____	_____	_____

3

THE BLUELINE CORPS

Whether they stay at home or lead the rush, defensemen are expected to perform their duties selflessly. They have to play the point as expertly as they clear out the opposition from their goalie's crease, blocking shots on goal with their bodies and taking hits to make the turnovers. This quiz is devoted to hockey's hard-working defensive corps.

(Answers are on page 25)

3.1 Which defenseman has the NHL's all-time highest plus/minus rating for one season?
A. Bobby Orr
B. Brian Leetch
C. Larry Robinson
D. Mark Howe

3.2 Who did the "Big Three" on defense play for?
A. The Edmonton Oilers
B. The Washington Capitals
C. The Montreal Canadiens
D. The Boston Bruins

3.3 How many times has veteran defenseman Rod Languay broken his nose?
A. Never
B. Twice
C. 5 times
D. 10 times

3.4 Which defenseman has scored the most regular-season goals in NHL history?
A. Denis Potvin
B. Ray Bourque
C. Paul Coffey
D. Bobby Orr

3.5 Which Hall of Fame defenseman wore a cape onto the ice before the opening face-off?
A. Emile "Butch" Bouchard
B. Eddie Shore
C. Brad Park
D. John "Black Jack" Stewart

3.6 Why did Bobby Orr wear sweater No. 4?
A. Rookies were given the lowest available number.
B. He was No. 4 with the Oshawa Generals.
C. Four is Orr's lucky number.
D. Coach Harry Sinden felt defensemen should wear low numbers.

3.7 Which trio of defensemen became the first to each score 20 goals for one team in a single season?
A. The Oilers' Paul Coffey, Charlie Huddy and Kevin Lowe
B. The Capitals' Kevin Hatcher, Sylvain Côté and Al Iafrate
C. The Bruins' Bobby Orr, Dallas Smith and Don Awrey
D. The Canadiens' Serge Savard, Larry Robinson and Guy Lapointe

3.8 Until 1992, when Roman Hamrlik was Tampa Bay's No. 1 pick, who was the last defenseman chosen first overall in the NHL draft?
A. The Bruins' Gord Kluzak
B. The Rangers' Brian Leetch
C. The Nordiques' Curtis Leschyshyn
D. The Oilers' Paul Coffey

3.9 How many goals did Brad Marsh score during his 15-year NHL career (1086 games)?
A. 23
B. 123
C. 223
D. 323

3.10 Which defenseman in the 1920s was suspended by *his own manager*?
A. Boston's Eddie Shore
B. Ottawa's King Clancy
C. Montreal's Sprague Cleghorn
D. New York's Ching Johnson

3.11 How many times have NHL teams produced *two* 20-goal scorers among their defensemen in one season?
A. 5
B. 10
C. 20
D. 40

3.12 As of 1992–93, which defenseman has scored the most points in professional hockey?
A. Bobby Orr
B. Mark Howe
C. Chris Chelios
D. Paul Coffey

THE BLUELINE CORPS
Answers

3.1 A. Bobby Orr.
Larry Robinson gave it a valiant try in 1976–77 when the
Canadiens lost just eight games all season. But even his
awesome +120 plus/minus rating couldn't equal Orr's
1970–71 mark of +124. Orr's rating is almost unbeliev-
able, considering the League's best player and leading
plus/minus man in 1992–93, Mario Lemieux, had a +55.
The best rating by a forward is Guy Lafleur's +89 in
1976-77. Orr is, and probably always will be, the standard
against which all good defensemen measure their hockey
skills.

3.2 C. The Montreal Canadiens.
The old sports saying "Offense wins games; defense wins
championships" was proven true time and again by the
"Big Three" on the Canadiens dynasty teams of the
1970s. Very big both in size and playmaking abilities, the
defensive trio of Serge Savard, Larry Robinson and Guy
Lapointe gave Montreal the balance, speed and muscle to
completely control the game in any zone on the ice. No
team before or since has ever boosted *three* all-star rush-
ing defensemen. Just ask Ken Dryden, who, stuck in his
familiar goalie pose, often watched the action from the far
end of the rink.

3.3 D. 10 times.
In 15 seasons of stick whacks, sharp elbows and face-
plants into the boards, Languay's beak has suffered its
share of breaks. The first one, the All-Star blueliner
proudly admits, came from Mr. Elbows himself, Gordie
Howe.

3.4 C. Paul Coffey.
Coffey's 330 career-goal mark is safe from Potvin (310 goals in 15 seasons) and Orr (270 goals in 12 seasons) but Bourque is moving into position, scoring 19 goals (compared to Coffey's 12) in 1992–93 for a career total of 291 goals — just 39 goals short. In Coffey's best year, 1985–86, he netted 48 goals, another NHL record for defensemen.

3.5 B. Eddie Shore.
Shore played in the Roaring Twenties and Dirty Thirties, a hockey era that witnessed great changes not only to the rules but in the marketing of the game. When Eddie Shore of Qu'Appelle, Saskatchewan blew into Boston in 1926, the Bruins knew they had themselves a gate attraction who could play skilled hockey *and* check, punch and scrap with the best of them. The Bruins indulged press and public alike — and their fast-rising star's flair for the unusual. After the warmup skate, with all the players on the ice, the Garden's house lights were dimmed, a spotlight appeared and out skated Shore, outfitted in a black and gold cape, blowing kisses to the tune of "Hail to the Chief" over the loud-speakers. Boston fans went wild while the opposition cringed at the antics of the NHL's first major marketing phenomenon.

3.6 D. Coach Harry Sinden felt defensemen should wear low numbers.
When Orr arrived at Bruins training camp in 1966, he was handed No. 30 and then No. 27 before Sinden settled on a low number — one traditionally reserved for the blueline corps. Orr, happy with any sweater number, soon made No. 4 *the* defenseman's jersey for a generation of fans.

3.7 B. The Capitals' Kevin Hatcher, Sylvain Côté and Al Iafrate.
The first time an NHL team ever produced three 20-goal scorers among defensemen was in 1992–93 when Iafrate (25 goals), Côté (21 goals) and Hatcher (34 goals) teamed up to provide Washington with extra firepower up front after a series of trades and injuries hurt the forward lines. The Capitals' defense corps all chipped in to become the highest-scoring defense in NHL history, tallying 95 goals, 29% of Washington's total goal output (325 goals) for 1992–93.

3.8 A. The Bruins' Gord Kluzak.
Only a handful of defensemen have ever been selected first overall; among them are Denis Potvin (1973), Rick Green (1976) and Rob Ramage (1979). But 1982 proved to be a banner year, with four of the first six draft positions going to defensemen. Boston picked first and selected Kluzak, a defensive star from the WHL with a big heart and bad knees. In nine seasons he struggled through . countless knee operations before being forced to quit in 1991. The entry draft made 1992 another exceptional year as three of the top five positions were swept by defensemen, including Tampa Bay pick Roman Hamrlik, the first non–North American defenseman ever chosen first overall.

3.9 A. 23.
Marsh was the archetypal journeyman. With little natural talent, he has had to work harder than most players to stay in the League. In 15 seasons with five teams, Marsh scored only 23 goals, every one of them a testament to his work ethic. His dogged efforts brought him to the 1993 All-Star game, where, ironically, he scored a goal.

3.10 C. Montreal's Sprague Cleghorn.
Cleghorn was perhaps the best defensive defenseman of his era. But when he held a grudge, it turned into an ugly self-serving vendetta irrationally carried to a point of absolute disregard for either his own hockey skills or the talents of his teammates. Cleghorn's red flag was the Ottawa Senators, a team that had dropped him in 1921. He exacted his revenge each time his new team, the Canadiens, played them, even with the Stanley Cup on the line. His undoing was a full-blown crosscheck to the face of Ottawa defenseman Lionel Hitchman, which knocked Hitchman out cold. Cleghorn was banished from the match. His own manager, Leo Dandurand, was so shocked by Cleghorn's viciousness that he decided not to wait for the League to take action and suspended him for the duration of the playoffs.

3.11 A. 5 times.
Teams seldom expect defensemen to be prolific goal scorers. After all, that's not what the position demands. In NHL history only five clubs have iced tandem 20-goal scorers on defense.

THE NHL'S 20/20 DYNAMIC DEFENSE DUOS

Team	Season	Players	Goals
Montreal	1974–75	Guy Lapointe	28
		Serge Savard	20
Edmonton	1982–83	Paul Coffey	29
		Charlie Huddy	20
Calgary	1987–88	Al MacInnis	25
		Gary Suter	21
Winnipeg	1991–92	Phil Housley	23
		Fredrik Olausson	20
Washington	1992–93	Kevin Hatcher	34
		Al Iafrate	25
		Sylvain Côté	21

3.12 B. Mark Howe.

Howe has been playing professional hockey, both as a forward and a defenceman, since 1973–74, when he joined his dad, the legendary Gordie Howe, on the WHA Houston Aeros. If Mark inherited anything from his father, who played 31 seasons, it was Gordie's herculean strength and endurance. While the average NHL career lasts 4.7 years, Mark, 38, entered his 21st pro season (1993–94) with 504 points in six WHA seasons and 712 points in the NHL. Mark Howe's 1216 career point total should soon be overtaken by Detroit teammate Paul Coffey, who begins 1993–94 with 1201 points. Orr totalled 915 career points.

GAME 2

"PUCK NORM"

If the NHL handed out awards to teams whose fans created the best spectator signboards, the hands-down winner for 1992–93 would be the North Stars. Owner Norm Green gave Minnesotans much to campaign about once the rumours of a franchise move to Dallas became fact. Embittered hockey fans at the Met Center struck back, designing placards with slogans like "Puck Norm," "Norm, Get a Life" and "Don't Pull the Plug, Norm."

Let's give first-year honours of the Puck Norm Trophy to all North Stars supporters for their collective resolve and clever artwork in signboard civil disobedience. In this game, you might find the runner-up. The challenge is to match the hometown arenas (below) with the appropriate slogans (facing page). Each slogan heralds a specific hockey event in 1992–93.

(Answers are on page 115)

Ottawa Civic Centre
Detroit's Olympia
Winnipeg Arena
Minnesota's Met Center
Quebec's Colisée
Buffalo Memorial
  Auditorium

New York's Madison Square Garden
Tampa Bay's Expo Hall
Calgary's Olympic Saddledome
Pittsburgh's Civic Center
Los Angeles' Great Western Forum
Toronto's Maple Leaf Gardens

1. _____ "Merci, Eric!"

2. _____ "Hey, Chicago! Wake Up and Smell the Coffey!"

3. _____ "Norm Suck$"

4. _____ "He's Baaaaack!" *or* "Simply the Best!"

5. _____ "Russian Heavyweight Title Fight: Mogilny vs. Bure"

6. _____ "Winning Is Fun"

7. _____ "Kick Ice!"

8. _____ "Don't Mess with Mark"

9. _____ "Welcome Back, Wayne"

10. _____ "52-53-54, Bossy's Record Is No More!"

11. _____ "**Da Outrageously Unquestionably Greatest Ice hockey Enforcer.**"

12. _____ "Welcome Back, Bob" *or* "There's a New Sheriff in Town!"

4

"HE CAN'T HOLD JOEY'S JOCKSTRAP!"

The quote. Sports figures have long delivered some of life's best lines — if not words to live by, at least ones worth repeating. Pull out your notepads; here are a few for the record.

(Answers are on page 34)

4.1 Who was Adam Oates referring to when he paid Joe Juneau this compliment: "He can't hold Joey's jockstrap"?
A. Eric Lindros
B. Felix Potvin
C. Teemu Selanne
D. Bruins equipment manager Ken Fleger

4.2 Which NHL team's dressing room is graced with the inscription "You play for the emblem on the front, not the name on the back"?
A. The Philadelphia Flyers'
B. The Los Angeles Kings'
C. The Vancouver Canucks'
D. The Buffalo Sabres'

4.3 When Conn Smythe said "I'm not a drinking man, but I know if you pour too much water in your whiskey, the whiskey gets weaker," what was he referring to?
A. League expansion
B. Longer regular-season schedules
C. Million-dollar player salaries
D. Prolonged play stoppages for TV commercials

4.4 Before Alexander Mogilny defected in 1989, a fellow Soviet player told him: *"Vsevo khoroshevo."* What does it mean?
A. "Meet lots of American girls."
B. "Best of luck in your new life."
C. "Kick ice — don't take any bad dives."
D. "Live long and prosper."

4.5 Who was Detroit manager Jack Adams referring to when he remarked "Geez, whoever saw one ambidextrous guy beat another ambidextrous guy before?"
A. Bobby Hull and Jacques Plante
B. Maurice Richard and Terry Sawchuk
C. Max Bentley and Turk Broda
D. Gordie Howe and Bill Durnan

4.6 When Jeremy Roenick said "I'm surprised he wasn't in the toilet when I went to the bathroom," who was he talking about?
A. His 1993 playoff shadow, St. Louis's Bob Bassen
B. Ex-Chicago GM Mike Keenan
C. NHL referee Don Koharski
D. St. Louis Blues goaltender Curtis Joseph

4.7 Which enforcer said "It's not often a plumber gets to go to the grand ball" after being invited to the 1992–93 All-Star weekend?
A. Mike Peluso
B. Stu Grimson
C. Kelly Buchberger
D. Brad Marsh

4.8 Who posted "To you from failing hands we throw the torch; be yours to hold it high" in the Montreal Canadiens' dressing room?
A. Coach Dick Irvin
B. Manager Frank Selke
C. Manager Sam Pollock
D. Coach Toe Blake

"HE CAN'T HOLD JOEY'S JOCKSTRAP!"
Answers

4.1 **C. Teemu Selanne.**
If rookies were rated by the publicity they generate, Eric Lindros would have won the 1993 Calder — and every other award handed out by the NHL. But who can argue that Selanne didn't deserve *his* press coverage, considering his dazzling 76-goal rookie season? Joe Juneau's linemate Adam Oates, for one. Oates scoffed at the European's "one dimensional" play, compared to Juneau's "complete game" and plus/minus skills. "Everywhere you go, people are talking about Selanne. It's not fair for Joey," fumed Oates. In any other year, Juneau (102 points and +23) might have taken the Calder, but how do you win a rookie race against the Next One, Felix

34

Potvin (2.50 GAA in 48 games) and a Finn who explodes for 76 goals? It's obvious who carried the athletic support in Calder balloting in '92–93; pronounce his name "tee-moo" (132 points and +8).

4.2 A. The Philadelphia Flyers.

"Money doesn't live forever. But great moments do." The late coach Fred Shero was never at a loss for words or quotes, especially those inspirational messages he scribbled on a player's locker or on the Flyers' blackboard before each game. His best became Philadelphia's motto in perpetuity: "As a Flyer, you play for the emblem on the front, not the name on the back."

4.3 A. League expansion.

While improved rules and equipment have brought great changes to hockey, nothing has had more impact on the game in recent decades than expansion. In just seven years (1967–74), North American pro hockey exploded from the "Original Six" into a 32-franchise operation with two pro leagues. As owners scrambled to discover and sign the best players, the talent pool was depleted. Scoring records were broken, salary scales went through the roof, and physical intimidation reached the goon stage. Smythe's whiskey analogy was right on — at the time. In the 1990s, expansion is crucial to the NHL's future success in the U.S. Intrastate rivalries in Sun Belt states like California and Florida and the rebirth of the Stars in Texas have made the footprint of pro hockey in the U.S. significant enough to attract major network coverage and national advertising revenues. And Smythe probably never imagined his six-team "old boys' league" drafting 18-year-olds from Valkeakoski, Finland. Today, more than 17% of NHLers come from Europe, blended in to fortify the "whiskey" Smythe so carefully guarded.

4.4 B. "Best of luck in your new life."
At the 1989 World Championships in Stockholm, Mogilny asked teammate Sergei Fedorov to defect with him. Fedorov declined, stating he couldn't leave his family, but wished Mogilny "*Vsevo khoroshevo.*" Only a year later, after being drafted by Detroit, Fedorov joined Mogilny and Pavel Bure in the NHL. In Russian hockey circles, Bure-Fedorov-Mogilny were considered the successors to the famed KLM line of Krutov-Larionov-Makarov. Could they have resurrected Russian dominance in international hockey? As it was, their defections dealt another blow to the once-awesome Soviet hockey machine. As famed Soviet coach Anatoli Tarasov said, "We have no hockey players left — they're all working in Canada."

4.5 D. Gordie Howe and Bill Durnan.
Although baseball has many famous switch-hitters, hockey has produced few players who shoot both left and right. But Gordie Howe could, as could Canadiens goalie Bill Durnan, who, like all goalies of his era, wore identical gloves; but, unlike any other backstopper, he could switch his stick from hand to hand while catching with the opposite. Each glove functioned as both a blocker and a trapper. But no amount of equipment would stop hockey's greatest scorer on a breakaway. In a game in the late '40s, after banging a puck off the post, Howe wheeled around in front of the net, switched to his left hand and tucked the rebound past Durnan. And Jack Adams was there the first time "one ambidextrous guy beat another ambidextrous guy."

4.6 A. His 1993 playoff shadow, St. Louis's Bob Bassen.
Chicago won the 1992–93 divisional title but was stoned four straight in the first playoff round against the rejuvenated St. Louis Blues, who had finished the regular season 21 points back of the Hawks. Give credit to Curtis

Joseph's 174-minute shutout streak and Bob Bassen's scrappy checking, which held 50-goal man Roenick to just one point until he got a goal and an assist in the final game. Afterwards, a frustrated Roenick quipped: "They kept throwing [Bassen] back out there, throwing him back at me. Every time I turned around, he had a stick in my face. I'm surprised he wasn't in the toilet when I went to the bathroom."

4.7 B. Stu Grimson.
Grimson's heavy shot landed him a spot among the NHL's elite scorers in the skills competition during All-Star weekend. The Hawks' enforcer, who totalled 2 points and 193 minutes in 78 games in 1992–93, gunned a 97.7 mph blast that earned him the distinction as the fourth-hardest shooter in the old Campbell Conference.

4.8 A. Coach Dick Irvin.
If, as the saying goes, hockey is a religion in Quebec and the Montreal Forum its cathedral, then Irvin's homily about holding high the "torch" has proven not only inspirational but a cross to bear for the players who have followed such immortal Canadiens as Maurice Richard, Howie Morenz, Jacques Plante, Jean Beliveau and Guy Lafleur. These demigods of the famous CH are honoured along a stretch of dressing-room wall above poet John McCrae's famous words from "In Flanders Fields," which Coach Irvin borrowed and inscribed, in French and English.

FIFTY 50-GOAL SCORERS

Ever since Maurice "The Rocket" Richard entered hockey's pantheon by recording the NHL's first 50-goal season in 1945, the milestone has gone from an almost unattainable feat to the undisputed standard by which single-season offensive excellence is measured. Today, more than 130 NHLers have equalled or bettered the Rocket's mark.

Forty-nine 50-goal scorers, listed below, appear in the puzzle, horizontally, vertically, diagonally or backwards. Some are easily found, like Brett Hull; others require a more careful search. After you've circled all 49 names, rearrange the five leftover letters to spell our fiftieth 50-goal scorer, the oldest NHLer ever to record a 50-goal season. Who is he?

(Solution is on page 116)

Anderson	Goulet	Leeman	Richer
Babych	Grant	Lemieux	Secord
Barber	Gretzky	Loob	Selanne
Bossy	Hadfield	MacLeish	Simmer
Bullard	Hawerchuk	Martin	Simpson
Bure	Hodge	Messier	Stevens
Carpenter	Hull	Mogilny	Stoughton
Carson	Kehoe	Mullen	Trottier
Ciccarelli	Kurri	Neely	Vaive
Dionne	Lafleur	Nieuwendyk	Yzerman
Esposito	LaFontaine	Ogrodnick	
Gare	Larouche	Redmond	
Geoffrion	Leach	Richard	

```
              E O H E K
R D D D Y     N G R S Y N R S N V
I I N R K     O R E P K E U I A A
C O O O U     T O B O Z L E M M I
H N M C R     H D R S T L L P R V
A N D E R S O N G N A I E U F S E E
R E E S I H M O U I B T R M A O Z N
D E R U B C E S O C M O G I L N Y I
R N T E S A S R T K X U E I M E L A
A I H N T E S A S T M H L O O B U T
L E S N E L I C N A C L B Y L E E N
L U I A V P E A R Y E G O U L E T O
U W E L E C R T B R E I T T O R T F
B E L E N G I A A E H C U O R A L A
O N C S S N B C C K E G D O H U L L
S D A R E H C I R E M M I S E R A G
S Y M N O I R F F O E G N A M E E L
Y K U H C R E W A H H A D F I E L D
```

5

THE BIG BUCK$

Hockey's a game of checks and balances, whether you're grinding it out in the corners or mucking it up with lawyers and taxmen. They'll all tell you the better you play, the more you're worth — just don't forget to get a good agent. Audit these questions and try to break even. *(Answers are on page 43)*

5.1 Which NHL team has the biggest player payroll?
   A. The Los Angeles Kings
   B. The New York Rangers
   C. The Pittsburgh Penguins
   D. The Montreal Canadiens

5.2 How many No. 88 Flyers jerseys were sold in Eric Lindros's rookie season, 1992–93?
   A. 2000 to 3000
   B. 3000 to 4000
   C. 4000 to 5000
   D. More than 5000

5.3 Who is the NHL's highest-paid coach?
   A. Scotty Bowman
   B. Pat Burns
   C. Rick Bowness
   D. Mike Keenan

5.4 How much money was involved in the first Maple Leafs offer for the rights to Canadien Maurice Richard?
A. $75,000
B. $135,000
C. $500,000
D. $1 million

5.5 How much did Wayne Gretzky and Bruce McNall pay for the 1910 Honus Wagner trading card?
A. $110,000
B. $210,000
C. $310,000
D. $410,000

5.6 How much did Toronto's Wendel Clark earn in regular-season bonus money in 1992–93?
A. $25,000
B. $125,000
C. $225,000
D. $325,000

5.7 What happens to the money collected as players' fines?
A. The NHL contributes it to the Players' Association's pension fund.
B. The NHL puts it toward minor league hockey programs.
C. The NHL turns it over to the Hockey Hall of Fame.
D. The NHL uses it as an emergency fund for retired players and their families.

5.8 Which NHL club is the most valuable hockey franchise?
A. The New York Rangers
B. The Montreal Canadiens
C. The Detroit Red Wings
D. The Pittsburgh Penguins

5.9 In base salary, how much *less* did hockey thug Tie Domi make than Jets teammate Teemu Selanne in 1992–93?
A. $25,000
B. $250,000
C. $550,000
D. $750,000

5.10 How many NHLers earned at least $1 million in 1992–93?
A. 10 to 20
B. 20 to 30
C. 30 to 40
D. More than 40

5.11 Which NHL arena has the most advertising signs?
A. New York's Madison Square Garden
B. Toronto's Maple Leaf Gardens
C. Quebec's Colisée
D. Philadelphia's Spectrum

5.12 What were the 1992 Las Vegas odds on the Tampa Bay Lightning or the Ottawa Senators winning the Stanley Cup in their first NHL season?
A. 100 to 1
B. 500 to 1
C. 1000 to 1
D. 2500 to 1

5.13 Conn Smythe built Maple Leaf Gardens at the height of the Depression. Besides attracting initial investors, how did he raise the capital?

A. He set up a stock-sharing venture with construction workers.
B. He oversold seat capacity.
C. He used money from concession and beer sales.
D. He organized benefit games at the old Mutual Street Arena.

THE BIG BUCK$
Answers

5.1 C. The Pittsburgh Penguins.
Pittsburgh's seven-year, $42-million contract with Mario Lemieux skyrocketed the Penguins' payroll to the top of the NHL list at $15.2 million annually, ahead of the Rangers ($14.7 million), Los Angeles ($14.1 million) and Montreal ($13.1 million). In 1992–93 alone, Pittsburgh's payroll jumped $6 million — more than the entire payroll of the NHL's lowest salaried team, the Ottawa Senators, whose players earned a total of $5.7 million. It takes the Penguins 31 home games to meet their payroll, using revenues from ticket sales alone.

5.2 D. More than 5000.
During Lindros's first NHL year, Philadelphia fans bought 5023 No. 88 sweaters, or about four times as many as all other customized jerseys combined. In one three-week period alone, the Flyers sold 51 jerseys per day, or one every 12 minutes. The crush to buy a Lindros sweater was so great that the manufacturer ran out of

orange material for the 88s. How much would a Eric Lindros sweater set you back? $88.88 (U.S.).

5.3 A. Scotty Bowman.

Bowman is reportedly earning nearly $2 million with Detroit over two years, making him the NHL's highest-paid coach. That makes sense: Bowman, 59, is hockey's winningest coach, with 971 NHL victories, and six Stanley Cup championships. Keenan has a five-year, $3-million deal with the Rangers, and Burns earns $350,000 annually with the Maple Leafs. The salary scale tips the other way for Ottawa's Rick Bowness, whose yearly salary, $150,000, is paid in Canadian funds.

5.4 A. $75,000.

In the days when players made $5000 a year, $75,000 was an exorbitant offer, even for the Rocket. Toronto's Conn Smythe, who had publicly criticized Richard's backchecking, proposed the deal to the Canadiens' Senator Donat Raymond, who replied: "I have read that you say Richard won't backcheck... Does this mean that, if I get him to play coming and going, you would offer me $150,000?" Two years later Toronto tried to buy the Rocket's playing contract again, this time for $135,000. Still no dice.

5.5 D. $410,000.

Gretzky and McNall purchased the mint-condition 1910 tobacco card of the Pittsburgh Pirates' Honus Wagner for the unprecedented sum of $410,000, the highest price ever paid for any trading card. Adding on Sotheby's auction commission of 10% or $41,000, the final price tag totaled $451,000!

5.6 C. $225,000.

While some players get paid extra to score, the injury-prone Clark got bonus money in 1992–93 for just showing up. After all, in five previous years he averaged only 37 games per season! Clark's contract called for bonuses of $100,000 for playing 45 games, an additional $75,000 if he played 55 and $50,000 more if he appeared in 65 matches. The Maple Leafs' captain managed a career-high 66-game season and earned his $225,000 bonus (but missed an additional $100,000 when he failed to achieve 40 goals or 80 points). Clark scored 17 goals and 39 points for his base salary of $600,000.

5.7 D. The NHL uses it as an emergency fund for retired players and their families.

In 1992–93, the NHL collected supplementary discipline fines totalling $157,631, all of which was set aside to discreetly provide charitable assistance to retired players and their families.

5.8 C. The Detroit Red Wings.

According to *Financial World* magazine, which annually ranks the worth of North America's major-league sports franchises, the Red Wings are hockey's most valuable club at $87 million. That figure is well below the market value of the first-place Dallas Cowboys ($165 million) or the Toronto Blue Jays ($155 million) but richer than that of the Rangers ($76 million), the Canadiens ($73 million) and the Penguins ($53 million). Despite the Red Wings' 54th ranking overall, they lead all North American sports franchises when it comes to profit margins, at 50.7%. The reason? Detroit pays only $1.00 (U.S.) a year to rent Joe Louis Arena.

THE NHL'S TOP AND BOTTOM DOLLAR TEAMS
($million/1991–92)

1. Det	$87	9. Phil	$58	17. NJ	$47
2. Bos	$79	10. NYI	$55	18. Wash	$45
3. NYR	$76	11. Pitt	$53	19. Buff	$44
4. Mtl	$73	12. Clgy	$52	20. SJ	$43
5. LA	$71	13. St. L.	$52	21. Stars	$42
6. Chi	$67	14. Edm	$51	22. Winn	$35
7. Tor	$63	15. Que	$48		
8. Van	$61	16. Htfd	$48		

Source: Financial World

5.9 A. $25,000.
Excluding his $1.5-million signing bonus, Selanne's yearly base salary of $400,000 was only $25,000 higher than Domi's annual wage of $375,000. But then, Domi racked up 344 penalty minutes in 1992–93, compared to Selanne's paltry 76 goals.

5.10 D. More than 40.
The NHL has 42 millionaires, including Mike Modano ($1.95 million), Joe Sakic ($1.8 million) and Grant Fuhr ($1.6 million). The League's seven-figure salaries (including signing bonuses) range from $1.1 million for Dave Manson to $6 million for Mario Lemieux.

5.11 C. Quebec's Colisée.
The average NHL arena features 72 advertising signs, but at the Nordiques' home rink there are more than 100 signs, representing 46 advertisers. In fact, Le Colisée has more sports advertising signage than any of North America's 87 other professional stadiums and arenas! That's because rink boards offer the most ad space, and because the NHL fully endorses arena signage, even allowing product logos to be painted on the ice. Furthermore, Quebec is a one-sport town. Fans live and die by

their Nordiques, who consistently draw sellout crowds, in good and bad years.

5.12 D. 2500 to 1.
Las Vegas gave odds of 2500 to 1 to anyone who would bet the Senators or the Lightning would win the 1993 Stanley Cup. That means a $10 wager would have returned $25,000. The Rangers (who didn't even make the playoffs) had the best odds, at 3 to 1, followed by the defending Cup-champion Penguins, with 5 to 1 odds. Vegas oddsmakers aren't so generous for either the expansion Panthers or the Mighty Ducks in their first year, 1993–94, giving odds of only 500 to 1.

5.13 A. He set up a stock-sharing venture with construction workers.
After raising almost $1.5 million, Smythe was still $200,000 short of capital. The Gardens would not have been built without a scheme he concocted to pay workers with stock certificates in lieu of cash. The gamble paid off for those who held onto their shares: the stock's value increased tenfold in 10 years.

Across

1. Barry Melrose's job
4. Too many players, "_____ in front of the net"
7. CBC's "Hockey _____ in Canada"
9. "Shift into second _____"
10. Short-handed, one man _____
11. "Two on _____"
13. "The puck took a bad _____"
14. "_____ problem!"
15. Opp. of away, "_____ home"
16. Fire_____ hockey
20. "_____-flung"
22. Play called back for _____
25. "Back _____ back"
26. "He _____ in team points"
27. "To _____ a playoff spot"
28. Getting hit, "Catch _____"
29. Negative, "_____ vibes"
30. "_____ donna"
31. Room to move; space
32. "Hold out for better _____"
35. Boston's famous No. 4
36. Teammates
37. _____-line pass
38. _____-weekly
39. Grind or "_____ it up"
40. _____ of ice
41. "_____'s no place like home"
43. "_____ on the lumber"
44. Part of boards, _____ boards
46. Away, "A _____ trip"
47. "_____ it in?"
48. "_____ a little harder"
49. "Make _____ break"
51. "Right _____ target"
52. Enemy
53. "_____ the defense"
54. "_____ crowd"
55. Boring, "A real _____er"
56. "Best _____ seven"
57. "Either them _____ us"

Down

1. Gallivanism: "A _____ shot"
2. "Cut down the _____"
3. "The puck _____ the post"
5. "Fast _____s, slow fists"
6. Gallivanism: equipment
8. "He shoots, _____ scores!"
12. "He's _____ the best player"
17. "Battle of _____"
18. "Don't give me the _____"
19. Chances to win or lose
20. An on-side is a "_____ play"
21. Referee raises his _____
23. PM hour; player's bedtime
24. _____ receipts
25. Art Ross _____
27. Mistake
30. Extra man, _____ play
33. Wage
34. "He _____ the puck ahead"
37. "_____ came to play"
39. "Get the _____ off our backs"
40. "_____ state of affairs"
41. "_____ the needle"
42. Quick goal at start of game, "an _____ goal"
43. Almost over, "_____ in the game"
45. Whistle down or "_____ the play"
47. "Back _____ shape"
49. Choose something else
50. All-_____
51. "Kill _____ the penalty"
52. Spectator
53. Old NHL, "Original _____"

48

HOCKEY TALK

(Solution is on page 118)

6

MASKED MEN OF THE CREASE

Goalies are to hockey what pitchers are to baseball: the most important players on the team. Pitchers throw 100 mph fastballs whereas goalies stop 100 mph slapshots, but both must be cool and extremely agile, with superb reflexes and concentration. In this quiz we throw down the gauntlet to size you up. Play the angles, and don't get caught out of position.

(Answers are on page 53)

6.1 **Who was the first NHL goalie to put a water bottle on top of his net?**
   A. Tony Esposito
   B. Pelle Lindbergh
   C. Grant Fuhr
   D. Gerry Cheevers

6.2 **Which active goalie with +250 games played has the best career winning percentage?**
   A. Andy Moog
   B. Patrick Roy
   C. Mike Vernon
   D. Tom Barrasso

6.3 **What kind of shot finally drove Jacques Plante to don the NHL's first mask?**
A. A Ted Lindsay wrist shot fired from point-blank range
B. A Bobby Hull slapper from the point
C. A Bernie Geoffrion mishap during a practice
D. An Andy Bathgate backhand flipped from the slot

6.4 **Who was the second NHL goalie to wear a face mask?**
A. The Canadiens' Charlie Hodge
B. The Hawks' Denis DeJordy
C. The Rangers' Dave Dryden
D. The Bruins' Don Simmons

6.5 **What do Tom Barrasso, Ed Belfour, Tony Esposito and Frankie Brimsek all have in common?**
A. Each goalie participated in a scoreless game.
B. Each goalie tied Terry Sawchuk's record for most shutouts in a rookie season.
C. Each goalie won the Vezina (top goalie) and Calder (top rookie) trophies in his first NHL season.
D. Each goalie won *Sports Illustrated*'s "Sportsman of the Year" honours in his rookie season.

6.6 **What goalies were drafted highest overall ever?**
A. Grant Fuhr, claimed by Edmonton in 1981
B. Tom Barrasso, claimed by Buffalo in 1983
C. John Davidson, claimed by St. Louis in 1973
D. Patrick Roy, claimed by Montreal in 1984

6.7 What goalie from the "Original Six" teams never played on an NHL expansion team?
A. Gump Worsley
B. Johnny Bower
C. Jacques Plante
D. Terry Sawchuk

6.8 When did "Shutout King" Terry Sawchuk record his first NHL shutout?
A. Between his 1st and 5th games
B. Between his 5th and 15th games
C. Between his 15th and 30th games
D. Not until his second NHL season with Detroit

6.9 Who is the youngest starting-goalie ever to win the Stanley Cup?
A. Patrick Roy
B. Terry Sawchuk
C. Grant Fuhr
D. Bill Ranford

6.10 When was the "trapper style" glove first worn by an NHL goalie?
A. 1918
B. 1928
C. 1938
D. 1948

6.11 Which goalie holds the NHL record for most points in a game?
A. Curtis Joseph
B. Ron Hextall
C. Jeff Reese
D. Grant Fuhr

6.12 What team introduced the two-goalie system?
A. The Toronto Maple Leafs
B. The New York Americans
C. The Detroit Red Wings
D. The Boston Bruins

6.13 The Flyers' Bernie Parent recorded the most wins in a season (1973–74), but which Boston Bruins goaltender holds the all-time NHL record for most *consecutive* wins in one season?
A. Gilles Gilbert
B. Ross Brooks
C. Tiny Thompson
D. Andy Moog

MASKED MEN OF THE CREASE
Answers

6.1 B. Pelle Lindbergh.
No exact date is on record, but Lindbergh did it first during the 1984–85 season. Few opponents objected, except for Edmonton coach Glen Sather who, smarting after a 4–1 loss to the Flyers in Game 1 of the Stanley Cup finals, sneered: "The next thing they'll be doing is getting room service for a chicken dinner out there." The water bottle was removed. The Flyers went on to lose the Cup. Coincidence?

6.2 A. Andy Moog.
In 496 games, Moog has compiled 279 wins, 128 losses and 57 ties for a .663 winning percentage, the best among all active NHL goalies. Drafted by Edmonton in the sixth

round, 132nd overall in 1980, Moog soon became an integral part of the Oilers' mission to become a dynasty, sharing equal duties with Grant Fuhr until 1987 when he was traded to Boston.

THE NHL'S TOP WINNING PERCENTAGE GOALIES
(1992–93)

Player	Wins	Losses	Ties	WP
1. A. Moog	279	128	57	.663
2. P. Roy	225	129	48	.619
3. M. Vernon	222	138	42	.604
4. G. Fuhr	275	174	65	.598
5. T. Barrasso	244	181	55	.566
6. R. Wamsley	204	131	46	.556
7. R. Hextall	159	126	36	.551

6.3 D. An Andy Bathgate backhand flipped from the slot.
The last shot ever to hit Plante's bare face was a Bathgate backhand which, according to the New York forward, was a "get even" shot, aimed deliberately at the Canadiens' goalie's face. Plante had levelled Bathgate earlier in the game, sending him crashing into the boards. Bathgate, fearing a separated shoulder, retaliated with a short backhand that struck Plante on the right cheekbone, cutting him badly. Ten minutes later, after some stitch work, Plante returned and faced the Rangers wearing the NHL's first goalie mask.

6.4 D. The Bruins' Don Simmons.
Once Jacques Plante donned hockey's first mask on November 1, 1959, it wasn't long before other goalies joined the so-called "mask brigade." Simmons, who had played his entire career without any face protection, waited just 2½ months before converting on January 10, 1960 when his Bruins blanked Toronto 4–0. Any lingering doubts about masks causing visibility problems quickly vanished.

Simmons posted a second straight shutout four nights later in New York, and all the nay-sayers fell silent.

6.5 C. Each goalie won the Vezina (top goalie) and Calder (top rookie) trophies in his first NHL season.
Only Barrasso (1984), Belfour (1991), Esposito (1970) and Brimsek (1939) have won double awards for regular-season play in their rookie years, although Terry Sawchuk and Al Rollins came close in 1951. Sawchuk won the Calder but was runner-up to Rollins in the Vezina — which evened things up, since Rollins was the Calder runner-up.

6.6 B and C. Tom Barrasso and John Davidson.
Because goaltenders tend to mature at a different pace than skaters, it's often difficult to assess a junior league goalie's full potential, so GMs rarely select them in early draft rounds. But some GMs have skated on thin ice, risking a high draft position on a gut feeling — with varying results. Barrasso and Davidson were selected in the first round, fifth overall, the highest entry-draft position ever for NHL goaltenders, by Scotty Bowman and Sid Abel respectively. Fuhr was chosen eighth overall in 1981; Trevor Kidd went 11th overall in 1990. Montreal took a chance on Michel Larocque in 1972, drafting him sixth overall, but waited till the fourth round in 1984 to select Roy, the 51st pick overall!

6.7 B. Johnny Bower.
Never have five netminders dominated a hockey era like Bower, Plante, Worsley, Sawchuk and Glenn Hall ruled the Fifties and Sixties. Their longevity is unparalleled in professional sports: they averaged 19 NHL seasons each! While Worsley (North Stars), Plante (Blues), Sawchuk (Kings) and Hall (Blues) moved among expansion teams, Bower was kept in Toronto, winning two Vezinas and keying the Leafs to four Stanley Cups. The influence of

this elite circle of NHL goalies lasted long after their playing days. They became the first goaltending coaches, instructing the next generation of backstoppers like Esposito, Dryden, Parent and Vachon.

6.8 A. Between his 1st and 5th games.

Sawchuk, the NHL's all-time shutout leader, notched his first of 103 career shutouts on January 15, 1950 when the Red Wings beat the Rangers 1–0. It was Sawchuk's fourth NHL game after being called up from Indianapolis to replace Harry Lumley (who was injured in a charity hockey game while playing as a forward). Before long the 20-year-old kid from Winnipeg got the call to start in nets every night for Detroit. Good move. Sawchuk won the Calder as top NHL rookie in 1951 and racked up 56 shutouts and a goals-against average of 1.93 during his first five seasons!

6.9 A. Patrick Roy.

The average age of netminders celebrating their first Stanley Cup is 25 years. Defying the law of averages are goalies like Fuhr (21.8), Sawchuk (22.4), Ranford (23.5) and Roy, who was a raw rookie of 20.7 years when he backstopped the Canadiens to a surprise championship in 1986. His electrifying post-season performance stunned the hockey world: he won 15 of 20 playoff games and posted a stingy 1.92 goals-against average (after a 3.35 GAA regular season), the best in the playoffs since Ken Dryden's 1.56 GAA in 1977 and a feat not since repeated. And as if winning the Cup weren't enough, Roy took home the Conn Smythe trophy as playoff MVP. He is the youngest player ever to do so.

6.10 D. 1948.
Chicago goalie Emile Francis took inspiration from his summer baseball-playing days in North Battleford, Saskatchewan to develop hockey's first "trapper style" glove. In a 1948 game against Detroit, Francis slipped on a baseball-style first baseman's mitt (Rollings's George McQuinn model with an added leather cuff) and began stopping pucks by picking them out of the air in much the same fashion as a ball player. Despite Detroit protests, referee King Clancy allowed Francis to continue using his "catching" glove, which soon became standard equipment for all goaltenders.

6.11 C. Jeff Reese.
Goalies are long remembered for game-winning saves, shutouts and win/loss records, but whatever Jeff Reese does next he will be immortalized for what happened on February 10, 1993. Backstopping Calgary in a 13–1 drubbing of the Sharks, Reese set the NHL point record for goalies, picking up three assists in one game. He admitted it was a "fluky" night. Lucky bounces and all, it was an unprecedented feat, even for the likes of Fuhr (most points in one season) or Hextall (most goals).

6.12 A. The Toronto Maple Leafs.
Although the two-goalie system wasn't formally adopted until the Sixties, it had long been discussed and debated. Managers argued that it was better to keep a goalie sharp in the minors than let him lose his edge while sitting on an NHL bench; some goalies felt it was too much to expect them to play 60 to 70 games, and play them well. Nonetheless, the Maple Leafs introduced an early version of the two-goalie system in 1950–51, with Turk Broda and Al Rollins sharing duties equally.

6.13 A. Gilles Gilbert.

Gilbert won a record 17 straight games in 1975–76. Interestingly, two other Bruin goalies are tied for second place, with 14 consecutive wins each: Brooks in 1973–74 and Thompson in 1929–30. So who's had the best winning streak since Gilbert's feat in 1975–76? Washington's Don Beaupre managed 14 wins in a row when he was with the North Stars in 1985–86.

GAME 4

MASTERPIECE MASKS

Goalie masks have come a long way since Bruins netminder Gerry Cheevers decorated his plain white mask with black stitch marks to indicate where pucks would have hit and cut his face. Today's goalies spend thousands of dollars on customized paint jobs that transform ordinary protective headgear into striking works of art. Embellished with team colours and emblems, they become symbols that readily identify the men behind the masks.

Match the NHL goaltenders and their famed mask designs.

(Answers are on page 117)

1. _____Toronto's Felix Potvin   A. Antarctic sea bird

2. _____Los Angeles' Kelly Hrudey   B. CH and "33"

3. _____Buffalo's Grant Fuhr   C. Fire

4. _____Pittsburgh's Tom Barrasso   D. Bird of prey

5. _____Montreal's Patrick Roy   E. Five Stanley Cups

6. _____New York's Mike Richter   F. Igloo

7. _____Quebec's Stephane Fiset   G. Crown

8. _____St. Louis's Curtis Joseph   H. Lady Liberty

9. _____Calgary's Mike Vernon   I. Cat's whiskers

10. _____Chicago's Ed Belfour   J. Musical notes

7

SHORT SNAPPERS

It's time to take a break from the heavy action and go surfing in the neutral zone. But don't let your guard down — these true or false questions could cheap-shot you with a blind-sided hit or, worse, leave you as trade bait in the next entry draft.

(Answers are on page 62)

7.1 **The Kansas City Scouts were the first NHL team to wear all-white skates.** True or False?

7.2 **The NHL's first 500-goal scorer, Maurice Richard, wristed that milestone marker into an empty net.** True or False?

7.3 **No defenseman has ever won the Art Ross Trophy as the NHL's leading scorer.** True or False?

7.4 **The first NHL penalty in Oilers franchise history was assessed to Wayne Gretzky.** True or False?

7.5 **Detroit once offered Marcel Dionne in a one-for-one trade for Canadiens goalie Ken Dryden.** True or False?

7.6 **Mario Lemieux is the NHL leader in penalty-shot goals.** True or False?

7.7 **Chicago's Bobby Hull and Stan Mikita never played on the same forward line.** True or False?

7.8 Foster Hewitt was hockey's first play-by-play announcer. True or False?

7.9 None of the NHL's past presidents has ever played or coached a day of hockey in his life. True or False?

7.10 Paul Coffey is the only defenseman to break the 500-goal mark. True or False?

7.11 More games have ended in victories than in ties at the end of five-minute overtime since its introduction in 1983. True or False?

7.12 An NHL team has never won a best-of-seven Stanley Cup final series by winning four road games. True or False?

7.13 Bobby Hull was the WHA's all-time leading goal-scorer. True or False?

7.14 No American-born player has ever won the Art Ross Trophy as the NHL's scoring leader. True or False?

7.15 On penalty shots, goalies stop the puck more often than shooters score. True or False?

7.16 Bobby and Brett Hull are the only father-and-son 50-goal scorers in NHL history. True or False?

7.17 Wayne Gretzky is the only player ever to win NHL scoring titles with two different teams. True or False?

7.18 Gordie Howe scored his last NHL goal in his last game. True or False?

SHORT SNAPPERS
Answers

7.1 False.
In 1967, with the eccentric Charles O. Finlay in charge, the California Golden Seals played in all-white skates. Within three months the team changed its name to the Oakland Seals and soon after dropped the white look for standard black skates.

7.2 False.
The Rocket slapped his 500th past Chicago's Glenn Hall, who was between the pipes for the big moment on October 19, 1957. Wayne Gretzky, Mike Bossy and Jari Kurri all scored their 500th goals into empty nets.

7.3 False.
Bobby Orr is the only defenseman ever to win the NHL's scoring race. Incredibly, Orr did it twice, once in 1969–70 (33–87–120) and again in 1974–75 (46–89–135).

7.4 True.
At 5:19 in the first period of Edmonton's first NHL game (October 10, 1979), Gretzky took the Oilers' first penalty, receiving two minutes for slashing.

7.5 True.
Before Dionne was offered to Los Angeles, Detroit put the star's rights on the trading block for Canadiens all-star goalie Ken Dryden. But Montreal knew better. Great goaltending wins more games than great scoring.

7.6 True.
Mario leads all NHLers in penalty-shot goals, scoring five times in six opportunities.

7.7 True.
From 1960 through 1968, Hull and Mikita owned the NHL scoring race, winning the scoring title seven times between them, yet the Blackhawks won only one Cup. To this day, Hull is critical of the Chicago coaching staff and thinks it was a mistake not to play the two forwards together, Hull on left wing and Mikita at centre.

7.8 False.
Toronto Daily Star reporter Norm Albert called the first play-by-play of a hockey game on February 8, 1923. Hewitt himself noted the fact in his *Star* column the next day, pointing out that Albert's presentation was "the inaugural broadcasting by radio for a hockey game play-by-play." Hewitt's voice wasn't heard on hockey's second broadcast, either. A Westerner, Pete Parker, called a game between the Regina Capitals and the Edmonton Eskimos of the WCHL on Saskatchewan radio March 14, 1923, eight days before Foster Hewitt's historic first broadcast from the Mutual Street Arena in Toronto.

7.9 False.
Of the NHL's five presidents only one, Red Dutton, played hockey. Before becoming the League's second president (1943–46), Dutton played with the Montreal Maroons and New York Americans (a team he eventually coached and managed until it folded in 1942). Dutton is best remembered for his rugged play — his 139 penalty minutes put him ahead of all NHLers in 1928–29.

7.10 False.
No defenseman has ever reached the 500-goal plateau, including Coffey, who leads all blueliners with 330 goals in 13 NHL seasons.

7.11 False.
In an average NHL season, of the 152 regular-season games that are tied after regulation time, 65% remain tied after overtime.

7.12 True.
Not only has no team ever won four road games in a final series, it's never happened in *any* best-of-seven playoff series.

7.13 False.
Hull potted 303 goals in 411 games, second to Quebec's Marc Tardif, whose 316 goals in 446 matches made him the WHA's all-time goal-scorer.

7.14 True.
No U.S.-born player has ever succeeded in winning the NHL's scoring title, although St. Louis, Missouri's Pat LaFontaine came close as Art Ross runner-up to Mario Lemieux in 1992–93.

7.15 True.
In one-on-one match-ups since 1983–84, there have been 96 goals scored on 217 penalty shots, giving goalies a 55.8% success rate to shooters' 44.2%.

7.16 True.
Brett inherited his father's patented bullet slapshot, and on February 6, 1990 the Hulls became the NHL's only father-and-son 50-goal scorers when the youngster popped his 50th, 28 years after Bobby recorded his first 50-goal season.

7.17 False.

Gretzky was not the first to win NHL scoring titles with two different teams (Edmonton and Los Angeles). But it's happened only once before. In 1917-18, the Canadiens' Joe Malone potted 44 goals in a 22-game schedule to become the NHL's first scoring leader. Two years later, he did it again with the Quebec Bulldogs, recording 39 goals in 24 matches. But neither the Great One nor anyone else has overshadowed Malone's real claim to fame, the record for most goals in one NHL game (see question 11.6).

7.18 False.

In Gordie's last *regular season* game on April 6, 1980 he scored a goal and an assist against Detroit, but five nights later his Whalers were swept by Montreal in a best-of-five playoff series. He racked up another goal and assist in the series but was held pointless in his last NHL game on April 11, 1980.

Across

1. '89 Flames SC manager, Cliff _____
6. '90 Oilers SC goalie, Bill _____
7. "The shooter let it _____"
9. '71 Habs SC coach, _____ MacNeil
10. Penguins' _____ Francis
11. '59 Habs SC-winning scorer, Marcel _____
14. '86 Habs, Mats _____
17. _____ Louis Blues
19. "He can hear with his _____"
21. 1907 SC champs, Kenora _____
23. "On thin _____"
24. "A bad _____ over his stick"
25. Scoreless tie
26. "Remaining _____ on clock"
27. Zeroed, _____ out
30. '84 Oilers SC goalie, Andy _____
31. '81 SC MVP, Butch _____
32. A short-_____ed goal
33. '89 Flames SC captain, _____ny McDonald
34. '89 Flames, _____ Loob
35. Home town of '67 champs
39. '74 Flyers SC coach
41. '80 SC-winner _____ Morrow
42. '69 Canadiens SC coach, Claude _____
43. Super_____
44. "He has _____ eyes"
47. "Going _____ in the zone"
48. One-time-_____
49. General _____
50. Lord Stanley of _____

Down

2. _____ Stanley
3. Isles SC-winner, John _____
4. Illegal stick work
5. U.S. team with most Cups
7. Spectator
8. #16 in illustration
12. '89 Flames SC winner, Joel _____
13. '61 Hawks, Eric _____
15. Stats page, score_____
16. _____ Dahlen
17. Penalty _____
18. _____-in the puck
20. '90 SC-winning city
21. Goon
22. Bad odds, a _____ shot
27. Brett, _____ of Bobby Hull
28. '66 Habs SC goalie, Charlie _____
29. Forward position
30. _____ advantage
32. '61 Hawks SC goalie, Glenn _____
33. '40 Rangers SC manager, _____ Patrick
36. "Win, lose _____ draw"
37. Rogatien Vachon's nickname
38. Leafs _____ Kennedy
40. Leafs SC coach, _____ Day
43. _____ing-eye pass
45. Extra period, abbr.
46. Shots _____ goal
47. '89 Flames SC-winning scorer, init.
48. " _____ behind the defense"

CROSSWORD #3

THE CHAMPIONS

(Solution is on page 119)

8

THE COACHES

When Detroit coach Jack Adams was faced with Toronto's "clutch and grab" defense system in the 1940s, he developed an offensive strategy called "dump and chase," designed to counteract the Leafs' close-checking style of play at their own blueline. Adams's method worked so well it became an NHL standard. This chapter focusses on the men behind the bench, a fraternity devoted to improving the calibre of their teams.

(Answers are on page 71)

8.1 **When did Scotty Bowman become the NHL's winningest coach?**
A. While coaching the St. Louis Blues
B. While coaching the Montreal Canadiens
C. While coaching the Buffalo Sabres
D. While coaching the Pittsburgh Penguins

8.2 **At the 1992 Toronto press conference introducing new coach Pat Burns, which player's name did the ex-Montreal coach get wrong?**
A. Wendel Clark
B. Peter Zezel
C. Doug Gilmour
D. Dave Ellett

8.3 What is the highest number of empty-net goals scored by one team in one NHL game?
A. 2
B. 3
C. 4
D. 5

8.4 What is the average length of a coach's term with one NHL team over the past 10 seasons?
A. 106 games
B. 136 games
C. 166 games
D. 226 games

8.5 How many press conferences does the coach of the Montreal Canadiens hold each season?
A. 50 to 100
B. 100 to 150
C. 150 to 200
D. More than 200

8.6 What do Mike Keenan and Scotty Bowman munch on behind the bench while coaching a game?
A. Licorice
B. Ice cubes
C. Sugar cubes
D. M & Ms

8.7 What NHL tough guy suffered an on-ice, near career-ending injury in 1969, only to return to action and later become an NHL coach?
A. Scotty Bowman
B. Ted Green
C. Al Arbour
D. Terry Crisp

8.8 How much time do coaches have to make a line change?
A. 8 seconds after the whistle
B. 12 seconds after the whistle
C. 16 seconds after the whistle
D. Technically, as much as they want

8.9 How many times, if ever, has an NHL coach won the Stanley Cup with three different clubs?
A. Only once
B. Twice
C. Three times
D. It's never happened.

8.10 Which coach (with minimum 600 regular-season games as a coach) won the most Cups in his playing days?
A. Toe Blake
B. Red Kelly
C. Al Arbour
D. Bob Pulford

8.11 When, if ever, was the last time a player-coach won the Stanley Cup?
A. During the 1920s
B. During the 1940s
C. During the 1960s
D. It's never happened.

8.12 Which NHL coach received the longest suspension ever for a game-related incident?
A. Ex-Chicago coach Mike Keenan
B. Ex-Los Angeles coach Tom Webster
C. Vancouver's Pat Quinn
D. Ex-Edmonton coach Glen Sather

THE COACHES
Answers

8.1 C. While coaching the Buffalo Sabres.
Bowman has been hockey's winningest coach since December 1984, when his Sabres defeated the Blackhawks for his 691st career win, surpassing Dick Irvin's mark set in 1956.

8.2 C. Doug Gilmour.
After introductions by Toronto GM Cliff Fletcher, Burns, in front of the national media, pulled on a Leafs team jacket and said: "I don't know the players very well...ah...there's *Darryl* Gilmour and I've always been a Wendel Clark fan." Burns learned "Darryl's" true identity soon enough. Under Burns, Doug Gilmour became Toronto's hottest player in 1992–93, scoring a team-record 127 points — 10 points more than the Maple Leafs' former record-holder and other famous Darryl, Darryl Sittler. With Gilmour's help, Burns coached Toronto to their best season win-record (44–29–11) in the 76-year history of the club. (Yes, there is a Darryl Gilmour. He plays for Phoenix in the Kings' system.)

8.3 D. 5.
You're the coach. It's the last game of the regular season. Your team, the Canadiens, is fighting for the final playoff berth. You need either a tie or at least five goals to avoid elimination. With Montreal down 3–2 in the third period, Chicago's Pit Martin connects twice in less than four minutes. The score: 5–2. The clock reads 10:44. Henri Richard looks over his shoulder at you and says: "It's like a bad dream." What would you do? Desperate times call for desperate measures. That's what Habs coach Claude Ruel figured on April 5, 1970. Win, lose or

71

draw, three more goals would get the Canadiens into the playoffs. It was a slapstick finish to Montreal's season, as Ruel pulled Rogie Vachon on every face-off and the Hawks capitalized each time, scoring five empty-net goals in eight minutes. It's the only time in 45 years the Canadiens missed the playoffs. And you want to be the coach!

8.4 C. 166 games.

According to an *Inside Hockey* survey, NHL coaches average two seasons, or 166 games, behind the bench before getting axed. Between 1982 and 1992, there were 109 coaching changes among NHL teams. Pittsburgh and Minnesota had the most turnovers, with eight each, and Washington, the safest club to coach, only two tenures, split between brothers Bryan and Terry Murray. Among active coaches, the Islanders' Al Arbour has the longest current streak with one team, having coached 377 games.

8.5 D. More than 200.

The coach of the Canadiens gives more press conferences than the prime minister of Canada. During the nine-month hockey season, coach Jacques Demers faces a phalanx of lights, cameras and questions 238 times. Press conferences are held the day before every regular season game, after every game, to announce every trade and sometimes even a rumoured trade. Every time something happens to the Canadiens, it's news. The coverage is relentless, from training camp to the playoffs. *Le Journal de Montréal*, only one of Montreal's four daily newspapers, dedicates five pages of print a day, seven days a week, to the Canadiens. In no other NHL city does a coach's job depend on winning the Stanley Cup or on a press corps that regards itself as both a guardian and guiding star of that sacred trust, the tradition of *Les Canadiens*.

8.6 B. Ice cubes.
As a hockey tactician and motivator, Bowman made a considerable impression on Keenan, who shares his mentor's custom of chewing chunks of ice during the game.

8.7 B. Ted Green.
Oilers coach Ted Green was once one of the game's roughest players but when he battled with St. Louis's Wayne Maki in 1969, the ex-Bruins defenseman met his greatest challenge. In Green's book, *High Stick*, Phil Esposito describes what happened: "They were sparring over in the corner near the Bruins' goal when Maki went down on one knee. He got right up and hit Greenie over the head with the hardest part of his stick — at the bend where the shaft joins the blade. Greenie was down when I reached him, and he looked awful." Maki's stick smashed Green's skull. Bone chips had been driven into the brain area that controls speech and the movements of the left arm and leg. Green's comeback was extraordinary. Three delicate brain operations and 14 months of therapy later, Green was back skating on Boston ice. He ended his NHL career after the Bruins' 1972 Stanley Cup; Maki played until 1973.

8.8 D. Technically, as much as they want.
Section 2, Rule 18(e) of the *NHL Rule Book* states: "The Referee shall give the visiting team a *reasonable amount* of time to make their line change . . . ." Nonetheless, Bryan Lewis, director of officiating, says the unwritten rule followed by each official limits the time to eight seconds. "Referees don't carry stopwatches, but use their internal clocks to judge the limit," says Lewis. The home team coach, with the advantage of changing lines last before play resumes, cannot cause undue delay in icing his next line.

8.9 D. It's never happened.
Scotty Bowman (Montreal, Pittsburgh), Dick Irvin (Toronto, Montreal) and Lester Patrick (Victoria, New York) all coached two Stanley Cup-winning teams, but no one has ever done it with three NHL clubs. However, coach Tommy Gorman (Chicago, Montreal Maroons) deserves an asterisk beside his name for winning seven Cups with four different teams, including two championships back to back in 1934 and 1935 as coach and five more as manager with the old Senators (1920–21–23) and the Canadiens (1944–46).

8.10 B. Red Kelly.
Kelly gained more recognition on the ice than off it. He coached a lot of games (742 matches with Los Angeles, Pittsburgh and Toronto) with little success. But as a defenseman with Detroit he won four Cups in 12 seasons, only to be traded to Toronto by Red Wings boss Jack Adams, who figured the Redhead was washed up. In fact, Kelly went on to his most productive years. Under coach Punch Imlach, he moved from defense to centre, teaming up with Frank Mahovlich and Bob Nevin to win four Cups in the next seven years. Kelly's eight championships easily best Pulford's four Cups and Arbour and Blake's three Cups each.

8.11 B. During the 1940s.
Ebbie Goodfellow is the only NHLer credited as a player-coach on the Stanley Cup. He captained the Red Wings during the 1930s and became a playing coach under manager-coach Jack Adams in 1941. From then on, Ebbie made fewer and shorter appearances on the ice, especially after Adams was suspended indefinitely after fighting with a referee during the 1942 playoffs. Although Ebbie played in 1943, he scratched himself from the playoffs entirely, realizing he could be more help behind the bench than on the ice. Nevertheless, he

earned a place in hockey history: Ebbie Goodfellow, player-coach of the 1943 Detroit Red Wings, Stanley Cup Champions.

8.12 B. Ex-Los Angeles coach Tom Webster.
Webster was nailed for 12 games, the longest game-related suspension in League history for a coach, after showing his "displeasure" at a penalty call by hurling a player's stick at referee Kerry Fraser in November 1991. The stick grazed Fraser's skates. It wasn't the first tantrum for Webster, who was ejected three times the previous season, once for another bit of "sticky" business against Calgary, once for cursing at a referee and once for punching Doug Gilmour, a move that landed him a four-game suspension and a $5000 fine. Webster later called the Fraser incident "regrettable" and praised the referee for his "professionalism." During his 12-game absence, the Kings slipped from second to fifth in the Smythe Division.

GAME 5

AMERICAN FIRSTS

Although American-based teams outnumber their Canadian counterparts, the ranks of teams on both sides of the border, until recently, have always been filled with Canadian talent. Today, Americans make up nearly 17% of all NHLers. In this quiz, find the U.S.-born players that reached the following milestones first. *(Answers are on page 117)*

Gordie Roberts   Neal Broten   John LeClerc
Frank Brimsek   Leo Dandurand   Rod Languay
Bob Carpenter   Brian Lawton

1. _____ 1st U.S.-born 50-goal scorer.

2. _____ 1st American goalie to win the Vezina Trophy.

3. _____ 1st U.S.-born coach to win the Stanley Cup.

4. _____ 1st American to play 1000 NHL games.

5. _____ 1st American chosen first overall in the NHL draft.

6. _____ 1st U.S.-born player to record 100-point season.

7. _____ 1st Vermont-born hockey player to make the NHL.

8. _____ 1st American defenseman to win the Norris Trophy.

9

WHEN PUSH COMES TO SHOVE

There have been some pretty good fights on the ice over the years. But today's tough guy had better be able to play some hockey, too; otherwise he'll be trading jerseys instead of punches. In this quiz we go toe to toe for a few rounds of misconduct. Pass the smelling salts. *(Answers are on page 80)*

9.1 Who said, "I don't want to get into a war of words, but, if he wants one, I've got more lines than he has teeth. And he hits like a butterfly, anyway"?
A. Bob Probert
B. Gino Odjick
C. Tie Domi
D. Todd Ewen

9.2. What song did the organist play after a bomb exploded at the Montreal Forum on the night of the famous Richard Riot in 1955?
A. The Platters' "Smoke Gets in Your Eyes"
B. Jackie Wilson's "Lonely Teardrops"
C. Percy Faith's "My Heart Cries for You"
D. Connie Francis's "Who's Sorry Now?"

9.3 How much money was Mark Messier fined for a stick-swinging altercation with Ulf Samuelsson in 1993?
A. $545
B. $2545
C. $15,545
D. $25,545

9.4 Who is considered the NHL's first enforcer?
A. Detroit's Ted Lindsay
B. Boston's Ted Green
C. Montreal's John Ferguson
D. Chicago's Reggie Fleming

9.5 Who was St. Louis's Lee Norwood talking about in 1992 when he said, "I wrestled a circus bear when I was 20 at the Pennsylvania state fair and that bear was not as strong as this kid"?
A. Quebec's Owen Nolan
B. The Islanders' Darius Kasparaitis
C. Philadelphia's Eric Lindros
D. Detroit's Keith Primeau

9.6 Who is the NHL's all-time playoff penalty leader?
A. Dave Semenko
B. Dale Hunter
C. Dave "Tiger" Williams
D. Ron Hextall

9.7. Before Dale Hunter received his 21-game suspension in the 1993 playoffs, who held the NHL record for playoff-game suspensions?
A. Tom Lysiak
B. Ron Hextall
C. Ed Hospodar
D. Dave Semenko

9.8 How many penalty minutes have been assessed to goalie Ron Hextall since his rookie year in 1986–87?
A. 230
B. 330
C. 430
D. 530

9.9 Which mayor once threatened police action if brawls continued to take place in his city's rink?
A. Calgary's Mayor Ralph Klein
B. New York's Mayor Ed Koch
C. Boston's Mayor Ray Flynn
D. Montreal's Mayor Jean Drapeau

9.10 Only once in NHL history have fighting majors been handed out in an All-Star game. Which superstar was involved?
A. Gordie Howe
B. Bryan Trottier
C. Tim Horton
D. Bobby Clarke

9.11 What kind of penalty did Toronto's Glenn Anderson serve after scoring his 1000th career point in 1993?
A. Fighting major
B. Delay of game
C. Game misconduct for an obscene gesture
D. Unsportsmanlike conduct

9.12 What rivalry produced the so-called "Good Friday Massacre"?
A. The Battle of New York — Islanders vs. Rangers
B. The Battle of Alberta — Oilers vs. Flames
C. The Battle of Quebec — Canadiens vs. Nordiques
D. The Battle of the Patrick — Flyers vs. Penguins

WHEN PUSH COMES TO SHOVE
Answers

9.1 C. Tie Domi.
It's been a war of words for two seasons. Probert called Domi a goon and a dummy, then Domi spouted on about Probert "hitting like a butterfly." But the showdown match on December 2, 1992, proved who could really sting when the gloves were dropped. Just 37 seconds into the game ex-Rangers coach Roger Neilson sent Domi, who hadn't played in three games, out to line up against Probert. The inevitable happened. In the 30-second fight a flurry of 59 punches were thrown, with Probert connecting on more than half of his. Here's the computer punch count.

DOMI–PROBERT HEAVYWEIGHT TITLE MATCH		
	Probert	Domi
Punches thrown	38	21
Landed	22	7
Percent landed	58%	33%

9.2 C. Percy Faith's "My Heart Cries for You."
On the eve of the 1955 playoffs, during a Detroit-Montreal match, someone set off a tear-gas bomb in the Forum to protest the suspension (for the entire playoffs) of Maurice Richard, the pride and soul of French Canada, for hitting a linesman during a brawl. As putrid smoke filled the Forum, fans began their exodus and the organist, choking back his own tears, played "My Heart Cries for You."

9.3 D. $25,545.
With the fine based on his $2-million-plus salary, Mark Messier's three-day suspension for swiping his stick at Samuelsson cost him $25,545. Messier was retaliating after Samuelsson deliberately raked his stick up and down the Ranger captain's rib cage in a check against the boards. Messier, playing with a rib injury, responded with gloved-hand punches and a flick of his stick that caught Samuelsson's mouth and jaw, breaking two teeth. The Penguins defenseman dropped his gloves and stick, anticipating a fight, but instead Messier swung his stick "in a sweeping motion." Neither NHLer will ever likely be a Lady Byng nominee, but Messier, one of the NHL's best players, claimed that Samuelsson, one of the League's dirtiest, tried to reinjure him. Whoa! No kidding! For his part, Samuelsson was docked $8697.

9.4 C. Montreal's John Ferguson.
Until Ferguson arrived in 1963, no NHLer had ever been hired deliberately to act as an enforcer. There had been plenty of tough hockey players, like Lindsay, Green and Fleming, but Ferguson was the first designated on-ice policeman, taking on bigger and rougher opponents who menaced his smaller teammates. It was the idea of Sam Pollock, Montreal's astute general manager, who, after losing a few Cups in the early Sixties, went on a long search for someone to offer "protection" to players like Jean Beliveau and Henri Richard. After settling on

Ferguson, Pollock wasted no time in establishing the Canadiens' new on-ice force, inserting him between Beliveau and Bernie Geoffrion for the 1963–64 opener against Boston. Twelve seconds into the game, Ferguson grabbed Green's sweater, pulled it over his head and began pummelling the Bruins tough guy. Later in the game, Fergie scored two goals. Pollock couldn't have grinned wider. In eight years with the Canadiens, Ferguson helped win five Stanley Cups.

9.5 C. Philadelphia's Eric Lindros.
An 11-year NHL veteran like Lee Norwood should know better than to pick a fight with someone 35 pounds heavier and four inches taller than himself. But then maybe the circus bears he wrestled in Pennsylvania were kinder and gentler than the 6'5", 230-pound Lindros, who took Norwood apart on November 7, 1992. It was the Next One's first NHL fight. Small consolation for Norwood.

9.6 B. Dale Hunter.
Hunter leads all NHLers in playoff PIM, with 584 minutes in 126 playoff games, beginning with the Nordiques in 1981. And that doesn't include his worst infraction, a 21-game suspension (to be served in 1993–94) after he laid a blind-side check on Pierre Turgeon during the 1993 playoffs. The Islanders' forward had just scored a goal after a giveaway by Hunter in his own zone. In retaliation, Hunter drilled the unsuspecting Turgeon, who was in the process of raising his arms in celebration. Turgeon, the Islanders' leading scorer, hit the boards hard and sustained a separated shoulder, eliminating him from the next playoff round. Hunter and the Capitals were each fined $150,000, and Hunter was given the longest suspension for an on-ice incident in NHL history.

9.7 B. Ron Hextall.
Since 1979, the NHL has handed out 19 suspensions for violent incidents during the playoffs. Hextall, the only player since '79 to receive two playoff suspensions, was assessed an eight-game penalty for swinging his stick at Kent Nilsson's legs in the 1987 finals and, in 1989, a 12-game suspension for attacking Montreal defenseman Chris Chelios with his blocker. Hextall's 20-game total falls one short of Dale Hunter's 21-game suspension for a blind-side check on the Islanders' Pierre Turgeon in 1993.

9.8 C. 430.
In seven NHL seasons (1986–87 to '92–93) Hextall has amassed 430 penalty minutes, the highest for any NHL goalie ever (including the Islanders' madman, Billy Smith, who managed a season high of 54 minutes in '78–79). In comparison, Hextall collected more than 100 minutes per season in his first three years, but mellowed out following his 12-game suspension for a vicious attack on Chris Chelios in the 1989 playoffs.

9.9 C. Boston's Mayor Ray Flynn.
Prompted by a bench-clearing 1986 Bruins-Canadiens brawl that spread to fighting among fans in the stands, Mayor Flynn sent letters warning Boston team owners they had to "take effective action to strongly discourage incidents of violence." Otherwise, the mayor said, he would send the police onto the ice if necessary to stop the fighting. Boston fans were skeptical; team owners used doublespeak, saying something about a "disadvantage competitively"; and John Ziegler offered the weirdest response. "The subject is too trite to comment on," said the ex-NHL boss. Ironically, the Garden brawl was started by Canadiens goon Chris Nilan, a Boston native.

9.10   A. Gordie Howe.
Gordie still outdistances everyone for most All-Star appearances (23) but he earned another, albeit more ob-
scure, All-Star distinction. It happened in 1948, when
Howe was a 19-year-old hockey sophomore. According
to reports, "the game had plenty of bruising contact," and
when Howe was run into the boards by Toronto defenseman Gus Mortson, both players "swung wildly with their
bare fists," even though "players were instructed to avoid
injury." But that wasn't the young Howe's way. He'd take
a fighting major, even in an All-Star game.

9.11   B. Delay of game.
Neither Vancouver's electronic scoreboard nor the public address system recognized his historic achievement,
but Anderson's Toronto teammates certainly let everyone know, storming over the boards en masse to congrat-
ulate him on the third-period breakaway goal that
marked his 1000th career point. Referee Denis Morel
promptly whistled a two-minute delay-of-game penalty
at the Leafs bench. Anderson served the penalty, but
nothing could wipe the grin off his face after he became
the 36th NHLer with 1000 career points.

9.12   C. The Battle of Quebec — Canadiens vs. Nordiques.
Perhaps no two NHL teams have vented more mutual
spite than Montreal and Quebec; certainly no game better demonstrated that once-bitter rivalry than the melee
on Good Friday in 1984. As one report noted, it was "a
vendetta...that became frightening in its bitterness and
duration." For 35 minutes the fighting raged, clearing the
benches twice: at the end of the second period and the
beginning of the third. Bodies and equipment littered the
Forum ice. Officials scurried from skirmish to skirmish,
hopelessly tugging at sweaters to separate the comba-
tants. On the card: every dressed player. The main event
featured Louis Sleigher, who sucker-punched Jean

Hamel and put him out of the game; Chris Nilan, who ambushed a defenseless Randy Moller and pummelled his face with several blows; and Peter Stastny, who suffered a broken nose at the hands of Mario Tremblay. It was referee Bruce Hood's nightmare come true, made worse by the fact that the players who were serving game misconducts returned to the ice for the third period only to wage another free-for-all that even pitted brothers Dale and Mark Hunter against each other. When it was all over, 10 players had been ejected and 252 penalties called, for a total only 46 minutes short of the playoff record set by the Red Wings and Blues in 1991.

GAME 6

RAPPIN' AROUND

After the Blues evened up the 1993 playoff series with the Maple Leafs at three games apiece, St. Louis's Jeff Brown, looking ahead to the deciding game, waxed philosophical and said, "Funny things happen when you've got a bunch of golf courses staring you in the face." It's the kind of observation that athletes are famous for — at least for the moment. Brown was right, the fairways looked greener: his Blues were blown out by Toronto in Game 7.

Match the puckmen and their not-so-immortal truisms.

(Answers are on page 117)

Part 1

Bobby Orr	Dave "Tiger" Williams
Don Cherry	Pat Burns
Bobby Clarke	Keith Allen, Flyers executive

1. _____ "I don't want to be Coach of the Year, I just want to be coach *for* a year."

2. _____ "You don't have to be a genius to figure out what we do on the ice — we take the shortest route to the puck and arrive in ill humour."

3. _____ "I think anyone would remember if he was offered over 10% of a National Hockey League club."

4. _____ "Dougie Gilmour is the greatest hockey player in the world."

5. _____ "Violence. Violence. If one more reporter asks me about violence in hockey I'm going to kill somebody."

6. _____ "Them Penguins is done like dinner."

Part 2

Roger Neilson   Gump Worsley
Gary Dornhoefer   Herb Brooks
Wayne Gretzky   Philadelphia bumper sticker

1. _____ "Wouldn't it be a shock if a general manager said that they were keeping the coach and getting rid of the whole team because no one on earth could extract a decent performance from such a terrible collection of players?"

2. _____ "You know, I've held women and babies and jewels and money, but nothing will ever feel as good as holding that Cup."

3. _____ "Only God saves more than Parent."

4. _____ "[Stastny's contract is] the greatest heist since the Brinks job."

5. _____ "They were checking us so closely I could tell the brand of deodorant they were using."

6. _____ "The only job worse is a javelin catcher at a track and field meet."

10
WHO IS . . .?

Who is Lou Boudreau? According to Kings' coach Barry Melrose, one of the NHL's great quipsters, it's a name he wanted to use in his playing days because, well, he thought Lou Boudreau was just a great hockey name. And what about hockey's "Royal Family," "Freddy Charles" or "Flats & Heals"? Who are they? Here's a quiz to test how much you really know about the people, real or imagined, in a game that has its share of heroes and zeroes. *(Answers are on page 91)*

10.1 Who is the Finnish Flash?
A. Jari Kurri
B. Esa Tikkanen
C. Teemu Selanne
D. Jyrki Lumme

10.2 Who is the little boy Don Cherry picks up during the opening sequence of CBC's "Coach's Corner"?
A. A child actor
B. Patrick Roy's son
C. Don Cherry's nephew
D. An unidentified four-year-old Canadiens fan

10.3 Who is Debbie Wright?
   A. The NHL's first female TV analyst
   B. The NHL's first female goal judge
   C. The NHL's first female scout
   D. The NHL's first female goalie

10.4 Who is the NHL's all-time leading goal-scorer from Quebec?
   A. Guy Lafleur
   B. Marcel Dionne
   C. Mike Bossy
   D. Mario Lemieux

10.5 Who is hockey's "Royal Family"?
   A. The Howes
   B. The Patricks
   C. The Sutters
   D. The Richards

10.6 Who is Freddy Charles?
   A. The only goalie ever awarded the Lady Byng Trophy
   B. The L.A. Kings' national-anthem singer
   C. Eric Lindros's ex-agent
   D. Hockey's most-traded player

10.7 Who was the NHL's youngest captain ever?
   A. Vancouver's Trevor Linden
   B. New Jersey's Kirk Muller
   C. Detroit's Steve Yzerman
   D. Minnesota's Brian Bellows

10.8 Who is Lloyd Percival?

A. The logo designer of the NHL crest
B. The silversmith who cast the Stanley Cup
C. The author of the book that taught the Russians hockey
D. Don Cherry's tailor

10.9 Who is Terry Ruskowski?

A. The captain of more teams than any other NHLer
B. The first player to use an aluminum stick
C. The first NHLer fined for having long hair
D. The only player selected in both the 1967 and 1974 expansion drafts

10.10 Who is the only NHLer ever to sweep hockey's "Triple Crown," winning the Art Ross (top scorer), Hart (MVP) and Lady Byng (good sportmanship) trophies in one season?

A. Gordie Howe
B. Bobby Orr
C. Stan Mikita
D. Wayne Gretzky

10.11 Who are "Flats and Heals"?

A. An Islanders' TV comedy duo
B. The arena mascots for the Tampa Bay Lightning
C. A pair of basset hounds owned by NHL boss Gary Bettman
D. Manufacturers of orthopaedic inserts for hockey skates

10.12 Who is the "Gordie Howe" of the minor leagues?

A. Scott Gruhl
B. Guyle Fielder
C. Don Cherry
D. Willie Marshall

WHO IS...?
Answers

10.1 C. Teemu Selanne.
The Jets waited four long years to sign the Finnish super-star after drafting him 10th overall in 1988. Winnipeg showed the virtue of patience and the power of money, finally securing the free-agented rookie by matching Calgary's $1.5-million signing-bonus offer. The investment paid off. In 1992–93, the "Gretzky of the Fjords" smashed Mike Bossy's record for rookie-season goals, turned Peter Stastny's rookie point totals inside out and stole the NHL Rookie of the Year trophy from Eric Lindros. Credit ex-Jets GM John Ferguson and current GM Mike Smith for the flash of genius in picking up the kid known as the Finnish Flash.

10.2 B. Patrick Roy's son.
CBC's familiar opening to "Coach's Corner" features a barking dog (Cherry's bull terrier, Blue), Cherry himself standing on the Bruins bench with outstretched arms, and Cherry hoisting Jonathan Roy, Patrick's son, the little boy wearing the Canadiens sweater.

10.3 C. The NHL's first female scout.
Wright, 26, became the first woman to scout for an NHL team when the San Jose Sharks hired her for the 1992–93 season. In her beat-up Ford Tempo, Wright clocked the miles, scouting on average a game every night during the season in the talent-rich territory of Quebec, eastern Ontario and the northeastern United States.

10.4 B. Marcel Dionne.
Unlike many of his Quebec-born confreres, this Flying Frenchman never won a Stanley Cup during his 18-year career with Detroit, Los Angeles and New York from 1971 to 1989. But Dionne did make it to the Hall of Fame

91

and in grand style, recording six 50-goal seasons and eight 100-point years, and establishing scoring records unbroken until Wayne Gretzky's best years. In fact, only two players in NHL history have potted more goals than Dionne — Gordie Howe (801 goals) and Gretzky (765 goals). With 731 goals, Marcel heads a long list of NHL superstars from Quebec.

QUEBEC'S ALL-TIME GOAL-SCORING LEADERS

Player	Seasons	Regular Season		Playoffs	
		Games	Goals	Games	Goals
M. Dionne	18	1348	731	49	21
M. Bossy	10	752	573	129	85
G. Lafleur	17	1126	560	128	58
M. Richard	18	978	544	133	82
M. Goulet*	14	1033	532	93	39
G. Perreault	17	1191	512	90	33
J. Beliveau	20	1125	507	162	79
M. Lemieux*	9	577	477	60	52

Active player/current to 1992–93

10.5 B. The Patricks.

No single family has contributed more to the improvement and quality of hockey than the Patricks. As the game grew up, one generation of Patricks succeeded another, both on the ice and behind the scenes, changing the rules, the style of play and the organization, taking an almost ruleless game out of the dank, poorly lit arenas and turning it into one of North America's four major professional team sports. Brothers Lester and Frank built Canada's first artificial rinks, painted the first blue lines for offside calls, and introduced the penalty shot and playoff format. Lester's sons Lynn and Muzz coached and served as general managers in the NHL, as does Lester's grandson, Craig, who today continues to carry on the family's rich hockey heritage as GM of the Pittsburgh

Penguins. More than hockey directors or innovators, all the Patricks were players first; some were great, others ordinary, but each developed a view of the game from the face-off circle out. All five Patricks have won the Stanley Cup.

10.6 D. Hockey's most-traded player.
You won't find stats on Freddy Charles in any hockey guide — he's fictional! The name, coined by players themselves, is hockey slang for the trade term "future considerations", as in: "He was traded for Freddy Charles."

10.7 D. Minnesota's Brian Bellows.
Bellows, only a year out of the junior ranks, was named North Stars co-captain at 19.2 years old when captain Craig Hartsburg went down two games into 1983–84 with a knee injury that sidelined him for much of the season. The sophomore Bellows fulfilled all expectations, leading Minnesota with 41 goals and scoring 14 points in 16 playoff games. Linden was a tri-captain at 20.6, Yzerman at 21.6 and Muller at 21.8. All four players were among the top four picks overall in their respective drafts.

10.8 C. The author of the book that taught the Russians hockey.
Even though the first edition of Percival's *Hockey Handbook* was published in the 1950s, the *Handbook* is still considered the definitive technical book on the game. You have to read only the first few lines to see why: "Skating is to hockey what throwing is to baseball, what tackling is to football, or what footwork is to tennis. It is the most important fundamental. Our research has shown that in the average full-length game players skate from two to three miles. When poor line changes are used, players skate as far as four miles per game. Skating is what the player does most. It is the foundation on which every-

thing else is built." When the coaches who introduced the game to the Soviet Union read this, the *Hockey Handbook* became their bible. Percival's ideas on conditioning programs, precision-passing drills and coaching techniques inspired the Soviets to implement a brand-new approach to hockey — an approach virtually ignored by the NHL until our eyes were opened at the Summit Series in 1972. Percival, who was tutored by the legendary Knute Rockne of Notre Dame, applied scientific principals to coaching, training and performing in an effort to make the game faster and better. Wayne Gretzky, who never met Percival, unwittingly paid the coach his greatest compliment when he said: "We've learned more from the Soviets than they from us." Yes, Percival was the hockey genius we overlooked.

10.9 A. The captain of more teams than any other NHLer.
In NHL history only one player, Terry Ruskowski, has been a full captain on three different teams — and on the first three teams he played with: Chicago in 1980–81, Los Angeles 1983–84–85, and Pittsburgh 1986–87. His career numbers (426 points in 630 games) give little indication of his true value as a character player described by Penguins coaches in 1986 as "the heart of the team and an inspirational leader."

10.10 C. Stan Mikita.
Playing among superstars like Bobby Hull, Gordie Howe and Jean Beliveau, Mikita achieved something in 1966–67 never done before or matched since: he won the NHL's scoring title, most valuable player award, and good sportsmanship trophy in one season. Even more impressive is the fact that Mikita repeated this feat, winning the "Triple Crown" again the following year.

10.11 A. An Islanders' TV comedy duo.
Take a couple of Ontario boys, eh? Okay, so like, Islanders Glenn Healy (now of the Rangers) and Patrick Flatley. Give 'em their own big-time cable TV show in New York and you've got "Flats and Heals," a between-periods takeoff on SCTV's Bob and Doug McKenzie of "Great White North" fame. How's it goin', eh? Each week fans are treated to wacky homegrown spoofs, interviews and impressions. It's pure Canadiana, eh? So g'day, you hosers!

10.12 B. Guyle Fielder.
Fielder was the kind of player who liked to control the puck. That's the knock against him and, true or not, it prevented his rise to the NHL. Just the same, the 5'9", 165-pound Idaho native survived a hell-bent semi-pro career that spanned four decades and 26 seasons, its longevity surpassed only by that of Gordie Howe's NHL and WHA careers combined. But unlike Howe, he never got his skating skills up to the NHL standard, a fact confirmed after try-outs with the Blackhawks, Bruins and Red Wings. Playing most of his years in the old WHL, Fielder racked up impressive totals, dotted with league scoring records, MVP awards and numerous All-Star appearances. His minor league record is one for the books: 1951 points (460 goals, 1491 assists) in 1496 games from 1947 to 1973.

Across

1. Bruins "C," Phil _____
6. 1970s Stars "C," _____ Harris
8. Knock out, abbr.
9. Habs "C," The Rocket, init.
10. Devils "C," _____ Bridgman
11. Habs "C" '80s and '90s, init.
13. _____-end
17. LA and Wings "C" from 1970s (not Dionne)
20. "_____ are the Champions"
21. Flyers first "C," init.
22. 1970s Canuck "C," _____ Lever
24. Canucks' "Russian _____"
27. 1980s Bruins "C," init.
28. Ex-Flyer Tim _____
29. Retired Caps and Whalers goalie Mike _____
32. _____ "The Cat" Francis
33. Leafs "C," Darryl _____
36. Fast or "_____ decision"
37. _____ Ciccarelli
38. "Only one _____ back"
40. "_____-ending injury"
44. Canucks "C," _____ Smyl
45. "_____ minute of play"
46. Mighty Ducks' hometown
48. Extra period, init.
49. Area in front of net
50. Wayne once captained them
52. Canadiens' logo initials
54. English for *équipe*
56. Pl., Ed Belfour's nickname
58. "_____ in the hole"
59. 1989 Leafs "C," Rob _____
61. 1970s Leafs "C," Dave _____
62. Old jersey number for goalie
63. _____ Louis Blues
64. _____ waivers
65. Vicious stick swing

Down

2. Montreal "C," _____ Savard
3. 1940s Wings "C," init.
4. 1940s Leafs "C," init.
5. Scoreless tie
6. Flames "C," _____ Lysiak
7. Wings "C," Alex _____
12. Fault or _____ in the ice
13. Tampa's first-year top scorer, Brian _____
14. Warm-_____ drill
15. "Terrible" _____ Lindsay
16. Pens forward Bryan _____
17. Only NHLer to wear "C" 3 times on 3 clubs, full name
18. Wings "C," Steve _____
19. _____ Secord
23. "He made _____ contact"
25. 1993–94 Rangers coach
26. Penalty
30. America, init.
31. Jets "C," Thomas _____
34. Flyers "C," _____ Van Impe
35. "_____ the pines"
36. Ex-Jets wing, Doug _____
39. 1930s Bruins "C, " _____ Clapper
40. 1970s and '80s Bruins "C," Wayne _____
41. "It's _____ or nothing"
42. "_____ up time"
43. Bruins "C," _____ Bourque
45. _____ Hewitt
47. 1990s Rangers "C"
51. TV's old singing cowhands Roy Rogers and Dale _____
52. "The Professor," Ron _____
53. "Missing two front _____"
55. Blues "C" and Islanders coach, init.
57. Ice thug
60. Minnesota's _____ Centre

THE CAPTAINS

(Solution is on page 119)

11

A LEAGUE OF THEIR OWN

It's one of the NHL's all-time great sports stories. Only a few hours after completing radiation treatment for Hodgkin's disease, Mario Lemieux returned to the Pittsburgh Penguins' line-up. His team, which eventually finished the 1992–93 season 35 games above .500 (56–21–7), had just suffered through an 11–11–2 record during his absence. Half the season's losses occurred in those 24 games Super Mario missed. The power play was ineffective, too, plunging from 26% to 17%. This chapter is devoted to the NHL superstars, an exclusive group of athletes in a league of their own.   *(Answers are on page 101)*

11.1 As of 1992–93, who has scored the most goals in the fewest games?
A. Wayne Gretzky
B. Mike Bossy
C. Mario Lemieux
D. Brett Hull

11.2 Who is the fastest skater in the NHL?
A. San Jose's Mike Sullivan
B. St. Louis's Bret Hedican
C. The New York Rangers' Mike Gartner
D. Washington's Al Iafrate

11.3 Since the 1940s only two NHLers have ever led three different teams in scoring points. Which two players have accomplished such a feat? And has anyone done it in consecutive seasons?
A. Andy Bathgate
B. Doug Gilmour
C. Mike Gartner
D. Vincent Damphousse

11.4 Maurice "Rocket" Richard shot left-handed. What position did he play with the Canadiens?
A. Centre
B. Right wing
C. Left wing
D. All three forward positions, depending on linemates

11.5 Why was Pavel Bure's *first* 50th goal of the 1992–93 season disallowed?
A. Because Bure was caught using an illegal stick
B. Because of goalie interference
C. Because the net got knocked off its moorings
D. Because of a referee error

11.6 What is the highest number of goals scored by one player in one NHL game?
A. 6
B. 7
C. 8
D. 10

11.7 Wayne Gretzky leads the League in goals scored (92) in one season by a centre, and Brett Hull has scored more goals (86) than any other right winger. Who holds the record for goals scored by a left winger in one season?
A. Bobby Hull
B. Steve Shutt
C. Kevin Stevens
D. Luc Robitaille

11.8 How did the legendary "Newsy" Lalonde get his nickname?
A. He worked in a newsprint plant.
B. He was a part-time sports reporter in Cornwall, Ontario.
C. He made shin pads by stuffing used newspapers in his stockings.
D. He announced out-of-town sports scores in the dressing room between periods.

11.9 What NHL rookie holds the record for most goals in one playoff season?
A. Jeremy Roenick, Chicago, 1990
B. Claude Lemieux, Montreal, 1986
C. Pat Flatley, Islanders, 1984
D. Dino Ciccarelli, Minnesota, 1981

11.10 Teemu Selanne became the NHL's third rookie to score +50 goals when he broke Mike Bossy's record in 1992–93. Who is the only other rookie ever to hit 50 in his first season?
A. Mario Lemieux
B. Dale Hawerchuk
C. Wayne Gretzky
D. Joe Nieuwendyk

11.11 How old was Gordie Howe when he scored his 800th NHL goal?
A. 40
B. 44
C. 48
D. 52

11.12 Besides Wayne Gretzky, which NHLers have had 50-goal seasons with two different teams?
A. Jimmy Carson
B. Mike Gartner
C. Pat LaFontaine
D. Pierre Larouche

A LEAGUE OF THEIR OWN
Answers

11.1 C. Mario Lemieux.

Although Lemieux is way back in 23rd place on the NHL's list of the top 100 all-time goal-scoring leaders, in goals per game the Magnificent One ranks first, with 477 goals in 577 games (.827 average).

THE NHL'S TOP FIVE SNIPERS — GOALS PER GAME
(Minimum 400 games)

Player	Years	Games	Goals	Goals per game
M. Lemieux	9	577	477	.827
B. Hull	8	459	356	.776
M. Bossy*	10	752	573	.762
W. Gretzky	14	1044	765	.733
L. Robitaille	7	557	348	.625

Retired/current to 1992–93

11.2 C. The New York Rangers' Mike Gartner.
In the skills competition at the 1993 All-Star break in Montreal, Gartner blazed around the ice of the Forum in 13.51 seconds (about 25 mph). Sullivan, Hedican and Iafrate skated coast to coast to coast in the next-fastest times, all under 14 seconds.

11.3 A and D. Andy Bathgate and Vincent Damphousse.
Although a number of players have led two different teams in scoring points, sometimes in back-to-back years (Gretzky in Edmonton and Los Angeles), only Bathgate (New York, New York-Toronto and Pittsburgh) and Damphousse (Toronto, Edmonton and Montreal) can claim three scoring titles. Amazingly, Damphousse did it in consecutive years. In 1990-91, he led the Maple Leafs with 73 points; he was traded to the Oilers in 1991–92 and tallied a team-leading 89 points; and then the year after that, 1992–93, Damphousse finished first among the Canadiens with 97 points.

11.4 B. Right wing.
Although Richard shot left-handed, he played right wing. The Rocket's scoring skills were maximized when Paul Haynes, coach of the Senior Amateur Canadiens, moved Richard to his "wrong wing." The new position gave him more net to shoot at, and he developed a devastating backhand shot. The advice proved invaluable, launching Richard on an 18-year tear through the NHL, in the course of which he racked up a record 544 goals — including the first 50-in-50, in 1944–45.

11.5 D. Because of a referee error.
Bure's *first* 50th for Vancouver came after an iffy Jets goal on a Phil Housley shot, which struck the middle back pipe of the net. The puck zinged out so quickly referee Ron Hoggarth waved it off. Bure picked up the puck and

returned fire in a dazzling performance up ice, wristing a shot over a sprawling Rick Tabaracci. The video replay on the Housley goal proved the Jets had scored, and Bure's marker was disallowed. But a few nights later, on March 1, 1993, the Russian Rocket potted his *second* 50th, becoming Vancouver's first 50-goal scorer.

11.6 B. 7.
On a bitterly cold January night in 1920, Joe Malone of the Quebec Bulldogs stepped onto the ice in Quebec City and into the record books by scoring seven goals (including three in two minutes) against Toronto in a 10–6 win. Because of the freezing temperatures few fans were there to witness Malone's historic game, but no one has forgotten his NHL scoring record, still unbroken 70 years later. Many players have come close, most recently Darryl Sittler, who scored six goals for Toronto in 1976.

11.7 D. Luc Robitaille.
It was a long time coming, but sooner or later someone had to break Steve Shutt's single-season record for goals by a left winger. His 60-goal mark, set in 1976–77, withstood many challenges from snipers like Kevin Stevens (54), Charlie Simmer (56) and Michel Goulet (57), but it wasn't surpassed until 1992–93 (in an 84-game schedule) when Lucky Luc became the highest-scoring left winger in NHL history. After smashing Shutt's bench mark with 63 goals, Robitaille targeted Stevens's 123-point season record, notching four points for the Kings in Game 84 on April 15, 1993, for a total of 125 points. Bobby Hull's greatest NHL season was 1968–69, when he scored 58 goals in a 76-game schedule. What left winger has the best goals-per-game average for one season? Hull does (.763), barely edging out Robitaille (.750).

11.8 A. He worked in a newsprint plant.
"Newsy" came to hockey with printer's ink on his hands and a scoring touch that made him arguably the game's dominant figure for 30 years. He began playing hockey in Cornwall in 1905, moved through four pro leagues and ended up coaching the Canadiens. More than a brilliant scorer (446 goals in 334 games), Lalonde was one of hockey's roughest players, often cursed as "the dirtiest sonofabitch ever."

11.9 D. Dino Ciccarelli, Minnesota, 1981.
Something happened to the North Stars on their way to the Stanley Cup finals. That something was Dino Ciccarelli, the scrappy 5'10", 175-pound right winger who played half of 1980–81 in Oklahoma City before joining the Stars and rewriting the NHL record books. Ciccarelli scored 14 goals in 19 playoff games, including three goals in the Cup finals against the unstoppable Islanders. Although Minnesota lost the Cup, they found a winner in Ciccarelli, a hockey player whose career had been in doubt since his junior days, when he suffered a badly broken leg. Every NHL team passed on the Sarnia, Ontario native, except the North Stars. Ciccarelli didn't disappoint: he finished the playoffs sixth overall in scoring, equalling Wayne Gretzky. Although Roenick (11 goals in 20 games), Lemieux (10 in 20) and Flatley (nine in 21) have since tried, no one has eclipsed Ciccarelli, the unlikely rookie sensation of the 1981 playoffs.

11.10 D. Joe Nieuwendyk.
Joe's back-to-back 51-goal seasons with Calgary (1987–88, '88–89) established his reputation as a playmaker with a scoring touch on the power play. In his first season, fresh out of Cornell University, the kid from Oshawa, Ontario turned into the runaway favourite for Rookie of the Year, tallying 31 power play goals, three shy of Tim Kerr's all-time record. With all the attention focussed on

the Calgary rookie who was tearing up the league trying to break Bossy's rookie record of 53 goals, Nieuwendyk hit his worst slump at precisely the wrong time. He went scoreless in his last eight games and admitted the pressure got to be "too much." Although rookies Hawerchuk (45 goals) and Lemieux (43 goals) came agonizingly close to scoring 50 goals, Gretzky must have felt the most disappointment. The NHL ignored Gretzky's first-year 51-goal output because of his prior pro status in the WHA.

11.11 D. 52.
Howe was a 52-year-old grandfather when he scored his 800th NHL goal on February 29, 1980. Gordie's career spanned five decades and 32 seasons. In his 2504 games (NHL/WHA), he scored 1087 goals, adding 1545 assists for a total of 2632 points. Howe was the all-time NHL leader in each category (goals, assists and points) when he retired in 1980.

11.12 C and D. Pat LaFontaine and Pierre Larouche.
Although a handful of players have recorded multiple 50-goal seasons with one team, and a few, like Gartner (Washington 50, New York Rangers 49) and Carson (Los Angeles 55, Edmonton 49), have come close to scoring 50 goals more than once with different teams, only Gretzky, Larouche and LaFontaine have done it. While Gretzky notched +50 goals nine times with the Oilers and the Kings, Larouche managed it once with the Penguins (1975–76) and again with the Canadiens (1979–80). LaFontaine became the third and most recent two-team/50-goal scorer with the Islanders (1989–90) and the Sabres (1992–93).

A BRAND-NEW SEASON

The playoffs. After 84 regular-season games the most important season is just beginning. Consider this quiz your final playoff round before the Stanley Cup finals in the next chapter. To make it to "the show," match the numbers below with their corresponding clues.   *(Answers are on page 117)*

801	½	6	103	5	3
92	50	7	26	544	9

1. _____   Most frequently retired jersey number.

2. _____   Maurice Richard's career goal-scoring mark.

3. _____   Number of goals in a hat-trick.

4. _____   Number of NHL teams prior to 1967 expansion.

5. _____   Terry Sawchuk's all-time leading shutout mark.

6. _____   Gordie Howe's all-time leading goal-scoring mark.

7. _____   Most consecutive Stanley Cup championships.

8. _____   Most number of goals scored in one NHL season.

9. _____   Maximum allowable curvature of hockey blade in inches.

10. _____   Most goals ever scored by one player in a game.

11. _____   Number of NHL teams in 1993–94.

12. _____   Benchmark of offensive excellence— number of goals in one season.

12

GOIN' TO THE SHOW

During the 1993 playoff finals, scalpers were fetching $1700 (U.S.) for a pair of Stanley Cup tickets to see the Kings and the Canadiens do battle at the Great Western Forum. But what price can be put on seeing hockey's two best teams vie for the game's richest reward? In this final chapter we play for the silverware. No charge. *(Answers are on page 110)*

12.1 **Since the NHL expanded the Cup finals to a best-of-seven format in 1939, what has occurred least often?**
A. A four-game sweep
B. A five-game series
C. A six-game series
D. A seven-game series

12.2 **Name the only team in NHL history to win the Stanley Cup in the seventh and deciding game in *sudden-death overtime*.**
A. The Montreal Canadiens
B. The Edmonton Oilers
C. The Philadelphia Flyers
D. The Detroit Red Wings

12.3 In NHL history, only 10 netminders have won the Stanley Cup at least four times each. Which goalies have won the most?
A. Jacques Plante
B. Ken Dryden
C. Grant Fuhr
D. Billy Smith

12.4 Who played in the most playoff games without winning the Stanley Cup?
A. Steve Larmer
B. Brad Park
C. Brian Propp
D. Ray Bourque

12.5 How old is the youngest person whose name is inscribed on the Stanley Cup?
A. 7
B. 15
C. 16
D. 17

12.6 The Montreal Canadiens have made 35 appearances in the Stanley Cup finals. How many times has an NHL team defeated the Canadiens to win the Stanley Cup on Forum ice?
A. Once
B. 3 times
C. 6 times
D. It's never happened.

12.7 Who was the first player ever to hold the Stanley
Cup above his head after winning the playoff
finals?
A. George Armstrong
B. Howie Morenz
C. Ted Lindsay
D. Howie Meeker

12.8 How many times did the North Stars play the "Hey"
song during their drive to the Stanley Cup finals
in 1991?
A. About 4 times per playoff game
B. About 6 times per playoff game
C. About 8 times per playoff game
D. About 12 times per playoff game

12.9 How many players besides Bryan Trottier have won
multiple Stanley Cups with two different teams?
A. Trottier is the first and only one.
B. 2
C. 3
D. 6

12.10 Which Calgary player was credited with the goal
that Oiler Steve Smith scored on his own net in
the 1986 playoffs?
A. John Tonelli
B. Steve Bozek
C. Paul Reinhart
D. Perry Berezan

12.11 What NHL arena plays the Beatles' "Octopus's Garden" in the playoffs?
A. Boston Garden
B. Toronto's Maple Leaf Gardens
C. New York's Madison Square Garden
D. Detroit's Joe Louis Arena

12.12 Despite winning several Stanley Cups, Claude Provost is still not in the Hockey Hall of Fame. How many Cups did the Montreal forward win?
A. 3
B. 5
C. 7
D. 9

GOIN' TO THE SHOW
Answers

12.1 D. A seven-game series.
Players don't like going to the seventh game in the finals. In the 55 best-of-seven finals since 1939, a seventh and deciding game has been necessary only nine times (and only twice since 1967); home teams have won seven out of the nine Cups. There have been 15 four-game series, 16 five-game series and 15 six-game series.

12.2 D. The Detroit Red Wings.
It doesn't get any better than when one shot on net clinches the whole season and the Stanley Cup championship. And Detroit knows this better than any other team. In 1950, the Red Wings battled the Rangers into seventh-game overtime, winning at 8:31 of the second overtime

period. Then, four years later, they pushed the proverbial
envelope again, to a seventh-game overtime against the
Canadiens. And they won again. The only team ever to
win the Stanley Cup in a seventh game overtime, and they
did it twice! The heroes: Pete Babando (1950) and Tony
Leswick (1954).

12.3 A and B. Jacques Plante and Ken Dryden.
Plante and Dryden head this exclusive list of goaltenders,
having each backstopped the Canadiens to an incredible
six Stanley Cups, or 12 championships between them,
from 1953 to 1979! Fuhr's five Cups for the Oilers is the
next-best total, and Smith won four with the Islanders.

12.4 B. Brad Park.
In his 17-year career, Hall of Famer Brad Park went to
the Cup finals on three separate occasions (1972 Rangers,
1977 and 1978 Bruins) and lost all three times. His 161
playoff games (or about two complete regular seasons of
hockey) have almost been matched by Propp, the top
active player in this category, who's played in 160 playoff
games. Bourque's game total is 139; Larmer's is 107.

12.5 A. 7.
Inscribed in the silverplate at the bottom of a list of
hockey greats like Charlie Conacher, Joe Primeau and
King Clancy is the name of Stafford Smythe, the seven-
year-old team mascot and son of Conn Smythe, general
manager of the Stanley Cup champion 1931–32 Toronto
Maple Leafs.

12.6 A. Once.
Since opening its doors in 1924, the Forum has been
lucky for the New York Rangers (1928) and the Montreal
Maroons (1926 and 1935), both teams winning the Cup
on Montreal ice, but neither club beating the Canadiens,
who after 35 final appearances and 12 Stanley Cup wins at

home have allowed only one visiting team in almost 70 years to capture Lord Stanley's trophy on Forum ice. The Calgary Flames did the unthinkable in 1989.

12.7 C. Ted Lindsay.
The ritual was initiated by Ted Lindsay in 1950. The Red Wings had just defeated the Rangers in a hard-fought seventh final game that went into double overtime. Detroit's Olympia rocked in the uproar. In one spontaneous act, filled with emotion and pride, "Terrible" Ted lifted the Cup above his head in celebration and skated to the boards so Detroit fans could touch it. With that gesture, Lindsay began a tradition that endures today.

12.8 D. About 12 times per playoff game.
Gary Glitter's 1972 hit, "Rock and Roll Part 2" (a.k.a. the "Hey" song) was sung 125 times during Minnesota's 11 home playoff games at the Met Sports Center in 1991. North Stars fans, delirious over their team's playoff run, were belting out the "Hey" almost every five minutes of playing time. But there was no song in their hearts on May 25, 1991, when the Penguins embarrassed the North Stars 8–0 to win the Cup.

12.9 C. 3.
In 1992 Trottier became only the fourth player in NHL history to win multiple Stanley Cups with more than one team. Trottier's playoff record (Penguins/two Cups, Islanders/four Cups) moves him into an elite group whose other three members are Frank Mahovlich (Maple Leafs/four Cups, Canadiens/two Cups), Red Kelly (Red Wings/four Cups, Maple Leafs/four Cups) and Dick Duff (Maple Leafs/two Cups, Canadiens/four Cups).

12.10 D. Perry Berezan.
It's the seventh game of the Edmonton-Calgary divisional finals. With the score tied early in the third period, Flames forward Berezan dumps the puck into the Oilers' zone and heads to the Calgary bench. Rookie Steve Smith, being chased by Lanny McDonald, skates behind his own net and launches the puck towards teammate Glenn Anderson. But the cross-ice pass banks off Fuhr, parked at the edge of the crease, and goes into the Edmonton net. Berezan, the last Flame to touch the puck, is credited with the goal — one he didn't even see go in. Smith, who is celebrating his 23rd birthday, falls to the ice in shame and utter disbelief. The Flames hold the lead and scuttle the Oilers' dreams of dynastic glory and a third straight Stanley Cup.

12.11 B. Detroit's Joe Louis Arena.
Few arena songs have less in common with hockey than Detroit's playoff anthem, "Octopus's Garden." It's a stretch, but the Beatles' 1967 classic echoes a peculiar Red Wing tradition dating back to the 1952 Stanley Cup playoffs. One night in the first round against Toronto, a Detroit fan threw an octopus on the ice for good luck. The refs jumped, but the home-town crowd, though at first lockjawed, cheered wildly as the symbolic meaning of the slimy eight-legged creature became clear. Sure enough, eight straight games and Detroit had swept Toronto and Montreal to win the Cup. The tradition stuck, fuelled by two more Cups in the next three years. Since then, though, Detroit has slid into the second-longest losing stretch in Stanley Cup history (only the Rangers have done worse). Red Wing fans still throw their cephalopod charm at playoff time, but deep down they know it takes more than seafood and a tune to carry a championship team.

12.12 D. 9.

Claude Provost is the only NHLer who's ever won more than eight Cups and not been inducted into the Hall of Fame. Not that it guarantees admission, but nine championships in one career is remarkable. A record 12 members from the Canadiens' five-in-a-row dynasty (1956–60) became Hall of Famers, but Provost was overshadowed by the Maurice Richards and the Jean Beliveaus in the balloting, as he had been on the ice throughout his years of checking the likes of Bobby Hull and Gordie Howe.

SOLUTIONS TO GAMES

GAME 1: A TRIO OF STARS

Left Wing	Centre	Right Wing
1. Brent Fedyk	Eric Lindros	Mark Recchi
2. Clark Gillies	Bryan Trottier	Mike Bossy
3. Wendel Clark	Russ Courtnall	Gary Leeman
4. Joe Juneau	Adam Oates	Dmitri Kvartalnov
5. Bobby Hull	Ulf Nilsson	Anders Hedberg
6. Luc Robitaille	Jari Kurri	Tomas Sandstrom
7. Greg Gilbert	Christian Ruuttu	Dirk Graham
8. Geoff Courtnall	Cliff Ronning	Trevor Linden
9. Wayne Cashman	Phil Esposito	Ken Hodge

GAME 2: "PUCK NORM"

1. Quebec's Colisée. With Philadelphia in town, Nordiques fans mockingly thank Eric Lindros for the players dealt to Quebec in the trade with the Flyers.

2. Detroit's Olympia. At one of Coffey's first home games (against Chicago) as a Red Wing, Detroit fans welcome the NHL's top offensive defenseman.

3. Minnesota's Met Center. Fans lambaste owner Norm Green over his decision to move the North Stars franchise.

4. Pittsburgh's Civic Center. After a 24-game absence (11–11–2), Mario Lemieux returns to the Penguins' line-up, increasing Pittsburgh's offensive output by an average of 1.5 goals per game.

5. Buffalo Memorial Auditorium. With the Canucks visiting, Sabres spectators match up the NHL's top two Russian superstars, Alexander Mogilny and Pavel Bure, in a title showdown. In the 3–1 Canucks win, Bure outscores Mogilny; both players assist on all four goals.

6. Ottawa Civic Centre. The Senators, after being outscored by the opposition 108–41 in 21 winless matches, win their first game in 47 days. Ottawa fans go delirious.

7. Tampa Bay's Expo Hall. The Lightning's slogan is "Kick Ice!"

8. New York's Madison Square Garden. Rangers captain Mark Messier locks horns with coach Roger Neilson, who eventually is handed his one-way ticket out of the Big Apple.

9. Los Angeles' Great Western Forum. Wayne Gretzky makes his season debut in Los Angeles after missing 39 games with a herniated thoracic disc.

10. Winnipeg Arena. Before a sellout hometown crowd, Finnish sniper Teemu Selanne pots a hat trick against Quebec on March 2, 1993 to tie and break Mike Bossy's rookie goal-scoring record.

11. Toronto's Maple Leaf Gardens. An ingenious fan's acronym spells out D-O-U-G-I-E, for Toronto's "Unquestionable" superstar, Doug Gilmour.
12. Calgary's Olympic Saddledome. Detroit's Bob Probert plays hockey in Canada for the first time in four years after receiving permission from U.S. immigration authorities to re-enter the United States. Calgary fans give the Red Wings' tough guy a rousing "cowboy" welcome.

GAME 3: FIFTY 50-GOAL SCORERS

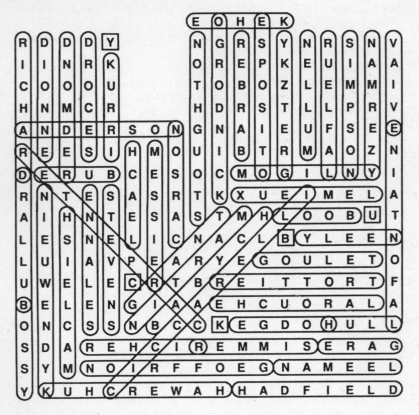

The Bruins' Johnny **Bucyk** was 35 years old and in his 16th NHL season when he scored goal no. 50 against Detroit goalie Roy Edwards on March 16, 1971. It was Bucyk's 69th game of the season.

GAME 4: MASTERPIECE MASKS

1. I   6. H
2. G   7. F
3. E   8. J
4. A   9. C
5. B   10. D

GAME 5: AMERICAN FIRSTS

1. Bob Carpenter of Beverly, Massachusetts became the NHL's first American-born 50-goal man on March 21, 1985.

2. Frank Brimsek of Eveleth, Minnesota won the top goalie honours as a member of the Boston Bruins in 1939.

3. Leo Dandurand of Bourbonnais, Illinois was coach of the Cup-winning Montreal Canadiens in 1924.

4. Gordie Roberts of Detroit, Michigan played game no. 1000 in 1992–93.

5. Brian Lawton of New Brunswick, New Jersey was selected first overall in the 1983 NHL draft.

6. Neal Broten of Roseau, Minnesota scored 29 goals and 76 assists for 105 points in the 80-game 1985–86 season.

7. John LeClerc of St. Albans, Vermont is the first and only Vermonter to crack the NHL.

8. Rod Languay, born in Formosa but raised in Boston, Massachusetts, won top defenseman awards in 1983 and 1984.

GAME 6: RAPPIN' AROUND

Part 1

1. Pat Burns
2. Bobby Clarke
3. Bobby Orr
4. Don Cherry
5. Keith Allen, Flyers executive
6. Dave "Tiger" Williams

Part 2

1. Roger Neilson
2. Wayne Gretzky
3. Philadelphia bumper sticker
4. Herb Brooks
5. Gary Dornhoefer
6. Gump Worsley

GAME 7: A BRAND-NEW SEASON

1. 9   7. 5
2. 544   8. 92
3. 3   9. ½
4. 6   10. 7
5. 103   11. 26
6. 801   12. 50

SOLUTIONS TO CROSSWORDS

**CROSSWORD #1:
STARTING LINE-UP**

**CROSSWORD #2:
HOCKEY TALK**

RT	Rick Tocchet
SD	Steve Duchesne
DW	Doug Weight
AK	Alexei Kasatonov
RC	Russ Courtnall
LB	Luciano Borsato
LR	Luc Robitaille
EL	Eric Lindros
BE	Bob Essensa
CT	Chris Terreri
DE	Dave Ellett
LM	Larry Murphy
MR	Mike Ricci
DT	Darren Turcotte
TE	Todd Elik
AM	Alexander Mogilny
IU	Igor Ulanov
VD	Vincent Damphousse
DR	Dominic Roussel
UD	Ulf Dahlen
JR	Jeremy Roenick
DA	Dave Andreychuk

CROSSWORD #3:

```
F L E T C H E R
O   O   O     E
R A N F O R D
D   E   K     W
    F L Y     I
H   A L   R O N   N
E   B O N I N     G
N A S L U N D   S T   T     E Y E S
R H   L     T H I S T L E S     D
I C E   F   H O P   O O   T I M E
R   E   S H U T   C   N   E     O
I   T M O O G     E   G O R I N G
C   H A N D   L A N       E     T
H A K A N   G   E     T O R O N T O
A   L     E   S H E R O   K E N
R U E L     S T A R   G O O D   O
D     O   D E E P     I         I T
M A N A G E R   P R E S T O N
```

CROSSWORD #4:

```
E S P O S I T O             T E D
  E     A   K O             O   E
M R                         M E L
  G C         B U T T           V
T E R R Y H A R P E R       W E
E   A   Z   L A   D O N         C
R O C K E T   D     T O         C
R   K E R R   L I U T   S       H
Y   E   M I L E   S I T T L E R I
R   S N A P   Y     E   E D I N O
U   M A N   D   C A R E E R   D
S T A N   F I N A L   A N A H E I M
K   I     O T   S L O T   Y   S E
O I L E R S   C H       T       S
W   V   T E A M   A   E A G L E S
S   A C E   R A M A G E   O     I
K E O N   R   O N E       T     E
I   S T   O N   T W O H A N D E R
```

DG   Doug Gilmour

SA   Sid Abel
TK   Ted Kennedy
MR   Maurice Richard
LA   Lou Angotti
TO   Terry O'Reilly
AA   Al Arbour

ACKNOWLEDGEMENTS

The following publishers and organizations have given permission for use of quoted material:

From "Iron Man of the Ice," by E.M. Swift, published in the *Sports Illustrated* Special Edition, Fall 1992. Copyright © 1992 Time Inc. All rights reserved. From *The Hockey News*, various excerpts. Reprinted by permission of The Hockey News, a division of GTC Transcontinental Publishing Inc. From *A Concise History of Sport in Canada* by Don Morrow, Mary Keyes, Wayne Simpson, Frank Cosentino and Ron Lappage. Copyright © Oxford University Press Canada 1989. Reprinted by permission of Oxford University Press. From *The NHL 75th Anniversary Commemorative Book*. Copyright © 1991 by the NHL and Dan Diamond and Associates. Reprinted by permission of McClelland & Stewart. From *Behind the Cheering* by Frank J. Selke. Copyright © Canada 1962 by Frank J. Selke. Published by McClelland & Stewart. Reprinted by permission of Frank D. Selke. From "Molson Hockey Night in Canada," a CBC Sports/Molstar Communications Presentation. Copyright © 1993 by The CBC. Reprinted by permission of The CBC. From *High Stick* by Ted Green with Al Hirshberg. Copyright © 1971 by Al Hirshberg and Ted Green. Published by Dodd, Mead & Company. Reprinted by permission of Ted Green. From *The Hockey Handbook* by Lloyd Percival. Copyright Canada, 1992, by Jan Percival. A Stewart House Book published by McClelland & Stewart. Reprinted by permission of McClelland & Stewart. From *The Stanley Cup* by D'Arcy Jenish. Copyright © 1992 by D'Arcy Jenish. Published by McClelland & Stewart. Reprinted by permission of McClelland & Stewart. From *Red Line* by Stan and Shirley Fischler. Copyright © 1990 by Stan and Shirley Fischler. Published and reprinted by permission of Prentice-Hall Canada Inc. From *The Sporting News*. Copyright © 1993. Reprinted by permission of The Sporting News. From

Gretzky: An Autobiography by Wayne Gretzky with Rick Reilly. Copyright © 1990 by Wayne Gretzky. Published in Canada by HarperCollins Publishers Ltd. From "Cracking the Ice" by Russ Conway. Published in 1991 by *The Eagle-Tribune* of Lawrence, Mass. Reprinted by permission of Russ Conway. From *The Gazette* by Tim Burke. Copyright © 1984. Printed and published in Montreal by Southam Inc. Reprinted by permission of The Gazette.

Care has been taken to trace ownership of copyright material contained in this book. The publishers will take any information that will enable them to rectify any reference or credit in subsequent editions.

The author gratefully acknowledges the help of Craig Campbell at the Hockey Hall of Fame, Brian Lewis and Garry Meagher at the NHL, Emile "The Cat" Francis, broadcaster Dick Irvin and CFCF-TV in Montreal, as well as editors Pat Ryffrank and Maja Grip, factchecker Allen Bishop, graphic artist Ivor Tiltin and crossword designer Adrian van Vlaardingen.